Revolution in Learning

This book was written with the assistance of a grant from Carnegie Corporation of New York. It is published by Harper & Row because of its significant contribution to thinking about current issues. The statements and opinions expressed in the book are solely the responsibility of the author.

MAYA PINES

Revolution in Learning

The Years from Birth to Six

54232

HARPER & ROW, PUBLISHERS

New York, Evanston, and London

LIBRARY OF CONGRESS CATALOG CARD NUMBER: 66-10657

A-T

To Michael and Daniel

CONTENTS

PREFACE

My first contact with the explorers of early learning came four years ago. On assignment from *Harper's Magazine*, I had gone to Hamden, Connecticut, to report on an experiment in which three-year-olds were said to be learning to read and write by typing on an electric "talking typewriter." Since I had a three-year-old of my own, I was intrigued by this project. But I was also highly skeptical. It sounded a bit like trying to teach dogs to play chess—they will never do it very well, and why bother?

For two days I watched some sixty children between the ages of three and six joyfully writing stories of their own, making up poems, exploring the typewriter keyboard, and reading paragraphs based on their own conversation. They did this as spontaneously as young children ask questions. I realized then that I had stumbled onto something far more important than the mechanical ability to read a few words. Evidently tiny youngsters could reason, invent, and acquire knowledge far better than most adults suspected. If they could learn this much through exposure to the talking typewriter for only half an hour a day, the potentialities of preschool children were almost limitless.

What about the next generation, then—what could I do for my own child, to help him develop to his fullest capacity? To my dismay, nobody could provide a rational, or even a sensible, answer. At the nursery schools I visited in New York City, most of the programs seemed based on the belief that the school could directly influence only the child's emotional and social development—not his mental growth. That was expected to occur automatically, following a sort of built-in time clock. Thus, "learning to get along with others" and "adjustment to the group" were everywhere the central goals. In practice, this meant that the school stressed either happiness and freedom of expression, or social graces and good manners, depending on its philosophy. The curriculum was almost always the same, with the largest amount of time reserved for free play with blocks, clay, and finger paints. At none of the schools did the teachers seem aware of the key role they could play in developing the children's intellectual potential.

The daily newspapers, on the other hand, were just beginning to report in detail on the great difficulties that the children of the poor were encountering in school. The problem of dropouts, the high rate of functional illiteracy, the discouraging results of remedial reading classes, the lack of readiness of so many first-graders—all these hard facts pointed to the need to do something earlier, before the child entered school at age six. Increasing amounts of research money were being channeled into pilot programs designed to fill this gap. And as new concepts evolved, it began to seem that they might be of use not merely to the children of poverty, but to all, including the exceptionally bright and the very dull.

At about the same time I learned of a study completed by Dr. Samuel Kirk, of the University of Illinois, which shocked me since I knew how difficult it was to help mentally retarded children. Back in 1957, photographer Cornell Capa and I had written a book on these children's urgent needs, based on a series of articles we had done for *Life* magazine. We had given relatively little emphasis to the earliest years. But shortly after our book came out, Dr. Kirk showed that when moderately retarded children were sent to special nursery schools at the age of three and kept there two or three years, many of them gained enough in IQ to take them out of the "retarded" group altogether.

Additional evidence of the impact of children's earliest environments came from Japan: A teacher named Shinichi Suzuki had trained thousands of youngsters, many of them between the ages of three and six, to play the violin with amazing musicianship. His method included much listening to records, for he wanted children to learn to make music just as they learned to speak. "Talent is common," he said, "but a favorable environment is not. . . . All human beings are born with great potentialities. We must investigate methods through which all children can develop their talents. In a way, this may be more important than the investigation of atomic power."

Any one of these developments would have been enough to whet my curiosity as a reporter, let alone as the parent of (by then) two preschool children. At the time, I was writing a book with microbiologist René Dubos, of the Rockefeller Institute, on the relationship between environment and disease. Dr. Dubos called his own research an example of "biological Freudianism" —he wanted to find out how biological characteristics would be affected by early exposure to various kinds of stress or stimulation. Such influences leave an indelible stamp on life, he concluded. Mice infected with certain bacteria at birth—the equivalent of a poor physical environment—never catch up in size with other mice of the same strain; they also show less resistance to radiation later in life. Guatemalan Indian children who are fed a protein-poor diet at home until the age of four and are then given an enriched diet in school never make up for their early loss in either physical or mental growth.

Fascinated by the way these bits of information fitted together, I decided to do a report on the growing number of projects involving some sort of "intellectual Freudianism"—research on how man's experiences in earliest childhood affect his intellectual growth. The Carnegie Corporation of New York gave me a grant to help me gather this material, which was scattered throughout the country. As soon as the book with Dubos was finished, I set out on an engrossing journey through selected universities, laboratories, and experimental schools, to learn what I could. The trip held many surprises—among them, a violent controversy among the experts themselves. It led me to various issues which I had never faced before.

When the time came to write it all down, I found I could not do as impersonal a job of reporting as I had done, for example, on disease. I had reached some conclusions on a subject that seemed to me extremely important. I felt that parents and teachers deserved to know more about the promise of early learning.

This book is addressed to everyone who cares about children and human intelligence. It is a passionate report on the discovery that we can produce more-intelligent as well as happier human beings by stimulating children to learn more during their earliest years.

I am deeply grateful to the pioneers of early learning who, despite exacting schedules of research, teaching, and writing, have given me their time with extraordinary generosity. Though my debts are numerous, that to Professor J. McV. Hunt of the University of Illinois takes special precedence. His willingness to share his encyclopedic knowledge and answer a reporter's endless questions fill me with awe. I am particularly indebted, too, to Professor Benjamin S. Bloom of the University of Chicago, Professor Omar K. Moore of the University of Pittsburgh, Professor Carl Bereiter of the University of Illinois, and Professor Burton White of Harvard University; patiently they explained their research, their thoughts, their conclusions. A great many other experimenters and teachers generously opened their doors to me, allowed me to observe their work, shared unpublished papers, suggested sources, or took the trouble to correct my errors. I thank all of them, and wish them well.

Chapter 1

THE BATTLEGROUND

MILLIONS of children are being irreparably damaged by our failure to stimulate them intellectually during their crucial years—from birth to six. Millions of others are being held back from their true potential.

Our severest educational problems could be largely solved if we started early enough. Yet we recklessly ignore an exciting and persuasive body of knowledge about how human beings learn.

This knowledge is just beginning to fit together solidly enough to call for action. Gathered from experimental projects that are scattered about the country, from research laboratories, and from scholars in various universities, it comes at a time when—for the first time in man's history—it makes sound economic sense to invest major efforts in the earliest years of human life.

Only a century ago, half the world's children died before the age of five—and this loss was considered inevitable. Through better nutrition and the control of infection, we now prevent the diseases that used to kill or cripple vast numbers of pre-

1

schoolers. At least in the affluent nations, every newborn child stands a good chance of survival. We approve of such public-health measures as putting extra vitamins into milk and flour and teaching mothers to sterilize milk bottles. But we continue to regard the intellectual crippling of young children as largely inevitable or as a private family matter in which nobody should interfere.

The scientists who would raise the nation's intelligence through early learning believe that few educators or parents have yet heard their message. As with public health, their methods could benefit the entire population. They could increase the talents and artistic involvement of all children. Poor children could be given specific training that would bring them up at least to the level necessary for success in school. Middle-class children might gain even more from early stimulation.

Any attempt to stimulate young children's intellectual growth in the United States, however, is likely to run into stiff opposition from the early-childhood Establishment: people trained in early-childhood education or child development and resentful of intrusion by other specialists who, they say, don't really *know* children.

A fierce, though largely undeclared war has been raging since the early 1960's between this Establishment, which is concerned primarily with children's emotional and social development, and the innovators, who emphasize cognitive, or intellectual, growth. The innovators include sociologists, linguists, mathematicians, philosophers and computer technicians, as well as many psychologists, all concerned with how young children learn to think and how best to help them.

The Establishment group believes in educating "the whole child": One should not try to teach specific skills in any organized sequence, but let the child learn from experiences that involve all aspects of his life: his emotions, his relations to other children, his fantasies, his surroundings, his actions. Thus, children are expected to learn color concepts simply by having colored toys around and occasionally hearing the teacher refer to them by color. They are supposed to learn number concepts by playing with blocks. Reading readiness is expected to come from recognizing their first names over their coat hooks. At best, these theories produce a special atmosphere of joy and well-being, from which the children come home all aglow, as after a good party. The Establishment is very indignant about what it calls "the vultures of experimental education poaching on this tender territory, forcing advanced curricula. . . ."

At the opposite pole, the "cognitive" group feels that by failing to take advantage of young children's real drive to know, the Establishment is wasting something very precious. Once past the sensitive period of their earliest years, children will never again learn with the same naturalness and ease. Teachers who prevent children from making the most of this period condemn large numbers of them to a downward spiral of failure. They condemn others to years of drudgery spent laboriously learning skills that might have come with ease at an earlier age, and that they might have been using to explore the world around them. Furthermore, happiness does not come from play alone. As one kindergarten teacher wrote—an exceptional woman who taught her five-year-old pupils to write, count, add, subtract, divide, use a simple microscope, and play the recorder: " 'Fun' is too weak a word to describe the elation, satisfaction, and inner peace that come from intellectual accomplishment." The cognitive group believes that such achievement plays a large part in good mental health.

I was unprepared for the violence of some of the experts' reactions. One noted child analyst told me that it was immoral even to write about the experimental programs, since parents might interpret such reports as advice. Others argued vehemently that if children did not learn, it was because of deep emotional problems, that it had nothing to do with teaching methods; accordingly, only therapy and a full spectrum of social services would help.

The two camps read different books, talked about different research problems, and attended different meetings. "Where did you find these people?" exclaimed an Establishment friend of mine when I told her whom I was planning to visit. When brought face to face, the two groups defended themselves with clichés.

"All children, being children, have the same needs," the Establishment asserted when anyone tried to devise special remedial programs for children from the slums. This seemed equivalent to saying that it mattered little whether preschool children were starving or well-fed—what all of them needed was a chance to express themselves through blocks and paint.

"Culturally deprived children need more stimulation," argued the cognitive types, confusing sensory stimulation—sheer amounts of light or sound, for instance—with symbolic stimulation, which implies some intellectual content or meaning.

"Why push them?" the Establishment responded to any attempt at putting some intellectual content into the preschool programs, as if they believed these children were too young to think —or that learning was something unpleasant, to be forced down a child's throat like castor oil.

"The child must learn how to learn," the cognitive psychologists asserted—sidestepping the burning issue of how this would be done (on which they all disagreed).

"They aren't ready to . . . before six," declared the Establishment. (Translation: The teacher isn't ready to teach them.)

It finally dawned on me that the split between these groups reflected more than different professional backgrounds; it revealed the different social classes of children each group most wanted to help. The old-line nursery school people were used to dealing with middle-class children whose parents taught them a great deal at home—or at least enough to cope with the demands of the first grade. The newer, cognitive types, on the other hand, urgently sought ways to arouse the sluggish brains of children raised by parents too poor, harried, or ignorant to teach them much that was relevant to school.

Thus it mattered little, academically, whether or not middle-class youngsters went to the existing nursery schools and kindergartens. Either way, they tended to do well in school; if they failed, the reasons were probably emotional or neurological rather than a lack of preparation. The large-scale failures of the poor, however, had at least one obvious reason: their total lack of preparation at home. Overcoming this lack would require a very different type of school.

A decade ago, Margaret Mead warned against "such fiascos as the application of nursery-school techniques—designed to free the overneat children of middle-class urban homes by letting them mess around with finger paints—to the deprived children from the disorderly, patternless homes of migrant workers. What these children really needed were the satisfying routines of the old kindergarten—itself an institution invented to deal with deprived children and which, when imported into middle-class education, had proved too mechanical and too routinized."

Only a few of the experimental programs dared to break away from the middle-class mold, however. One of the more striking ones I saw was run by two young men at the University of Illinois, in Urbana, who narrowly defined their academic goals for four- and five-year-old slum children, and then proceeded toward these goals one step at a time, in logical sequences.

It surprised me to find how modern and revolutionary the ideas that Maria Montessori first expressed around 1910 still sound—and how applicable they are to problems worrying so many educators today.

Most individualized of all was Omar K. Moore's "responsive environment" method, including his talking typewriter, on which young children could teach themselves to read and write, tracing their own paths to learning.

In various parts of the country, several other exciting pilot projects were going on. They showed how vastly we have underestimated young children's ability to learn, and how much even the brightest middle-class children are missing. Yet nobody was taking advantage of their findings. Their staffs often worked in isolation, hardly aware of what other researchers were doing. The majority of existing preschool programs, and particularly Project Head Start, pointedly ignored them.

The innovators' stiffest hurdle in their conflict with the Establishment was the problem of *proving* that their methods worked better. Unfortunately, the tools with which they tried to measure young children's progress were so crude that such proof was almost impossible. For lack of anything better, most educators fell back on the Stanford-Binet or similar intelligence tests, which they acknowledged to be both too broad and too dependent on verbal ability. Specific achievement tests could be given only after a child had learned to read and write. Until then, the various tests that were supposed to measure his ability to think, his reading readiness, his concepts of space, or other traits usually reflected entirely different factors—for example, the kind of speech the child heard at home. They also correlated badly with one another. A truly reliable battery of tests to measure young children's intellectual progress remains to be invented.

The battle also raged around theory. Many of the innovators' ideas seemed based on the work of Swiss psychologist Jean Piaget, who brilliantly described how children construct their changing image of the world out of ingredients supplied by their environment. Though Piaget's major books were first published in the

1930's, they had little impact in the United States at the time, being rediscovered only recently.

Another influential figure is Lev Vygotsky, a Russian psychologist of the same vintage, who died in the Soviet Union in 1934 and whose work has also just been rediscovered. The recent emphasis on children's language development can be traced right back to Vygotsky. American psychologists—relative newcomers to the study of cognitive growth—are only beginning to put their own stamp on the subject, largely through the use of computers.

Though at first I thought the battle would concern mostly children between the ages of three and six, I soon learned that it extended right back to the crib. The hottest area for research right now is not the earliest years, but the earliest *months* of life. Psychologists increasingly believe that the roots of intellectual curiosity are laid during these months. In a rich environment the child begins to get "kicks" out of learning soon after birth. If nothing arouses him, however, or all his attempts at learning are squelched, he will stop seeking this pleasure—to everyone's loss.

As Jerome Bruner wrote recently, "We get interested in what we get good at." Half the children in this country never have a chance to get good at anything, let alone become interested in it. Having failed to master basic skills early in life, they must either beat the system or flee from it, burying whatever talents they might have developed. Other children grow into the kind of college students whose thoughts, Sir Isaiah Berlin noted, "come higgledy-piggledy out of the big, buzzing, booming confusion of their minds."

The cognitive psychologists believe that the lives of all children could be made much richer if their abilities were developed systematically from the moment of birth. The idea is not to forget the other aspects of life—the children's vital emotional and social development, which go on simultaneously—but to give intellectual and artistic growth their proper places. By doing so, and by tailoring each child's intellectual diet to suit his needs, they hope to raise a nation of ever more differentiated, intelligent, adaptable, and creative adults, who will know how to make the best of both work and leisure.

At stake in the current battle is the future of America's 25 million preschoolers. The cognitive psychologists have shown several ways of increasing their achievement, but we have been unwilling to put their knowledge to use. A prime example of this unwillingness—and its consequences—can be found in the experience of Head Start.

Chapter 2

HEAD START

"FIVE or ten years from now, when the kids who've been through Head Start are found still at the bottom of the academic heap, the racists and know-nothings will have a field day," the young psychologist predicted gloomily.

Many researchers who recognize the full extent of the preschool problem share this young man's concern. For Project Head Start as it stands today—largely a summer project for underprivileged five- and six-year-olds who will enter school the following fall—can really help only those children who don't need it very much. To affect the hard-core cases it would have to act as a springboard for much more radical programs, including year-round classes with specific objectives for children of three and four. Most importantly, it would have to change the entire content and emphasis of its classes. So far it has failed to learn from the shortcomings revealed during its first summer, 1965.

Nevertheless, Head Start did put preschool education on the

map. It triggered such a vast outpouring of good intentions and energy, not to mention publicity, that poor children suddenly became much more difficult to ignore in their earliest years. Its size was staggering: 560,000 children attended programs in 13,400 centers that opened on a few months' notice in 2,500 communities during the first summer. Its hopes—and press releases—knew no bounds.

By summer's end, President Johnson proclaimed the experiment "battle-tested" and proven "worthy." As a result of the program, he said, more than half a million youngsters who had been on the road to despair were ready to take their places beside their more fortunate classmates in regular school. Press reports called it a "catch-up" program, implying that in eight weeks of summer it enabled the children of poverty to catch up with everything that middle-class youngsters had learned during their first six years. Everywhere, people told one another that it had been a great success. Hadn't the children adjusted well to the routines? Hadn't they enjoyed their contact with kind and understanding adults? Of all the Great Society's programs, this proved to be by far the most appealing, something no one would want to oppose—like motherhood.

Unfortunately, this sort of enthusiasm may cause the whole program to boomerang. If people are led to believe that the summer Head Start program can solve all of poor children's problems, or can even begin to solve such problems, they will become very angry when they see the lack of results. They may also refuse to provide what is really needed.

In fact, Head Start is a desperate, last-minute attempt to make up for deficiencies not in the child, but in the educational system. By pouring in people and services for two months before school, the system hopes to do without such people and services all year round. But it is too little, and much too late.

Head Start actually offers a combination of social work, preventive medicine, and indoctrination in the virtues of school. Since poor families commonly lack all three, Head Start often comes as a breath of hope and fresh air, a new contact with the promise of America. In this sense, it improves the children's chances of "getting along" in school. If a child can't hear his teacher, Head Start will discover it right away, and a hearing aid will be provided for him—hopefully, before the beginning of school. If he can't speak English, he'll learn enough key words to make life bearable in kindergarten or first grade. A youngster who is scared of going to school will lose some of the fears that might paralyze him for a whole year. One who is too aggressive may learn some control before getting into trouble with a regular teacher who, for reasons of self-preservation (twice as many children in her class, but not a single assistant), maintains firm discipline.

All these things are gains—and, in particular cases, they may be enormous gains. But they do not produce any real change in the children's understanding, language skill or ability to learn. By the age of five or six, slum children trail so far behind middle-class children that from an educational point of view they are already remedial cases. Improving their behavior is not enough. Mere "enrichment," such as field trips or clay modeling, is not enough. What they need is intensive, systematic training to bring them closer to the verbal and abstract level required for success in school. And this, with few exceptions, Head Start has not begun to provide.

Early in the summer, and again toward the end of the project, I visited several Head Start centers in the New York–Westchester area to get some idea of what they did provide. New York City's program was the largest in the nation; the Board of Education ran the majority of centers there, with a wide assortment of nonprofit organizations sponsoring the rest.

I soon learned that one could not really talk about *the* Head Start program, since each center was entirely different from the next. Those run by experienced and gifted teachers, such as Mrs. Lorelle Lawson, the director of a storefront Head Start center in a largely Negro and Puerto Rican neighborhood on New York's West Side, sometimes generated a certain radiance, that almost physical presence of good spirits and ease that comes only when a class really clicks. Here the sponsor was the Goddard-Riverside Community Center, a settlement house. After less than two weeks in the program, the children seemed bright-eyed and glowing. They obviously liked what they were doing—climbing on the armchair of a teacher as she read from "activity" books that called for patting the bunny or feeling a beard; going off on trips to the Empire State Building or Chinatown. There were fewer than four children per adult in this center—"and that's the way it should be," said Mrs. Lawson.

How each child spent his time at this center depended mostly on what he felt like doing. The children came together as a group only twice a day, for the park and for lunch-time.

The staff included a husky male volunteer—a college student on his summer vacation—who came to work each day with his Polaroid camera. One of his functions was to take pictures of the children while they were engrossed in various activities, so that these pictures could later be discussed in small groups. Since at least half the children in the center had no father, this young man meant a lot to them. Many of them were being raised by an old grandmother, I learned, or by a sister only a few years older than themselves. In one case, after her twelve-year-old sister had disappeared, a little girl was left in the day-time care of a seven-year-old.

Despite some outstanding successes, particularly in the way of "bringing out" children who seemed too quiet or sullen, the end of the program left glaring holes. "Their verbal ability seems stunted," reported one of the teachers. "I had them out for a walk the other day and we passed a big moving van. One of the boys shouted, 'Look at that big—' and then he didn't know what to call it, so he said 'street!' One of the girls was climbing up a hill and said, 'Isn't this sleepy!' She meant climbing makes you tired or sleepy. They just don't know the words. Yet the verbal level is the only way the school will deal with them. How can you expect these kids to read when they can't even talk?"

I watched an assistant teacher play picture dominoes with two little girls and try to make them say the names of the items on the pictures. "Do you have the cherry or the star?" she asked. "Do you have the heart?" But the girls just nodded or showed the pictures they had, usually without speaking. Sometimes one of them did not even understand the question, and then the teacher had to repeat it in Spanish.

Two other children busily rolled and molded some Play-dough, also without speaking. At the sand table—a long, waist-high table filled with sand—four boys were playing with toy trucks, which they ran over sand mountains and valleys, making the sound of motors and speaking loudly in Spanish. Under the table, two little girls collected the sand that had spilled over and quietly made mud pies with it.

Mrs. Lawson had put a lot of effort and thought into this center. She felt proud of its achievements, many of which involved helping the child's family over some major problem, and she worked overtime preparing long reports to various agencies, in the hope that these cases would be followed up. Yet she strongly felt the need for a different kind of program.

"We should start at age two!" she declared. "There should be some sort of program, whether it involves only the parents, or parents and children, or only the children. There could be a cooperative nursery school for every one or two buildings on a block—or at least someone who goes from house to house and talks to parents to explain what needs young children have." On the other hand, she did not want to "lift a natural responsibility from people. If we as a nation take full responsibility for raising children, then why are there parents? I'm very ambivalent about this."

A woman psychiatrist who had spent some time studying the children in this center on her own initiative, and to whom a few cases had been referred for possible treatment, put the matter more bluntly. "As a rule, I find that what they need is day care, not therapy," she said of the children who had been referred to her because of special problems. "Therapy is no substitute, it cannot take the place of life—it's like giving someone only vitamins, and no food! Better have rickets and remain alive than starve to death.

"One of the boys I was asked to see lives alone in a one-room apartment with his mother. She is not entitled to welfare because she receives an allowance of $120 a month from her husband, who's in the Army. Her dream is to buy herself another bed— the boy is nearly five years old now, and still sleeps in her bed. She'd like to work, to earn some money, but for that the child would have to go to a day-care center. And she can't find one that has space for him. Meanwhile, what is there to treat? Any child who has led that isolated a life with his mother is bound to be a little peculiar. And two hours a week of therapy can't serve as a substitute for what he needs all day."

In the next center I visited, I had a glimpse of what school must be like for an underprivileged child when, as often happens, he is placed in the hands of an inexperienced and poorly trained teacher. The scene was a Head Start center run by the school system in Harlem, and in fairness I must add that it was only the second week of the program.

I had heard this class all the way down the hall. "Stop screaming, boys!" an angry-looking young teacher shouted as I entered the room. Her voice barely carried over the clatter of blocks tumbling and the children's screams. A boy was sliding along the floor; he crashed into another child, who began to cry.

In an aside to me, the teacher explained: "This is supposed to be unstructured play—they're supposed to build what they like with the blocks. But some of these boys were discipline problems in kindergarten. William, for instance"—she pointed to the boy who had been sliding across the room—"his mother told me he'll be repeating kindergarten. My job is to sit on them and make them pay a little attention."

At this, William began to leap wildly from block to block across the floor, wielding a long wooden block and ramming things with it. In his path, all constructions collapsed and children fled. The large, airy room seemed filled with children and with shrieks. But, as I counted them later, there were only thirteen young children in the room, with one kindergarten teacher and an assistant.

As the two teachers tried to make the children put the blocks away, three boys pounded on the piano. "No!" cried the assistant teacher over the din, "I said, Put them away!" A hamster cowered in his cage. A little girl, unconcerned, went right on painting at an easel throughout the noise and commotion. But a boy who had been climbing a pile of blocks crashed down hard and started to wail. The angry-looking teacher crouched beside him, trying to comfort him. Then a Negro girl ran up to her and excitedly whispered something in her ear.

"Oh, my God!" cried the teacher. "With all my other problem children I got a new one today, and he's just run away!" She rushed out of the room. It turned out she had misunderstood—the new boy was found still in the room, indistinguishable in the melee. Instead, a tall, skinny girl was brought back, sucking her thumb. "Oh, she always cries when she's not getting

enough attention, and she never says anything," the teacher
told me disgustedly. "Sit down," she ordered the child. The tall
girl tried to run out of the classroom again, but this time the
teacher caught her. "I don't care if you cry, you've got to sit
down," she shouted, flinging her into a chair. At these words,
the girl buried her head in her knees and began to sob. They
were heart-rending, loud sobs. A few of the children gathered
around her to watch with interest, but each was ordered to take
his place around the table. The new boy, a Puerto Rican, did not
move. "Siéntase," repeated the teacher in Spanish, assuming it
was a language problem. "No," replied the boy, grinning, and he
went off to play at the other end of the room. The girl who had
run away was still sobbing.

"Now," the teacher said grimly, after nearly all the children
were seated, "let's sing!" And she turned on a scratchy folk-
song record whose words could hardly be made out: "This old
man . . . knick-knack on my shoe . . . knick-knack paddy-wack
. . ." The children seemed totally uninterested. The music was
alien to them, and they understood neither the words nor the
teacher's mechanical gestures—clap, open, shut. They began talking to each other or moving their chairs, drowning out the music.
"William, I said to *listen* now!" shouted the teacher. Finally she
gave up and turned off the record, ordering the children to wait
quietly until they got their juice.

"I thought we'd have some singing," she explained to me,
"but, as you see, they *won't* cooperate. They don't know how
to do things together." Meanwhile, the children were getting
bored just sitting there, waiting. One of them wandered off
toward the toys; he was brought back forcibly to sit down. The
assistant teacher had gone out of the room to fetch the juice.
Then one little girl started to chant softly, "We want juice! We
want juice!" This was taken up by the others, including the
recalcitrant William, and soon they were all chanting together

enthusiastically, "We want juice!" as if to disprove the teacher's comment about their ability to cooperate.

Finally the juice arrived, nearly 35 minutes late—nobody knew why it was late, said the assistant teacher who had been waiting for it all that time. Once again there were two adults for this group. "We're supposed to give them individual attention," explained the teacher. "Regular classes have only one teacher for twenty-five kids!"

To everyone's relief, the clock hand reached the appointed hour at last, and the class was over. One by one, the children were picked up by their parents or someone else. A bright-looking Negro girl of about eight came for her younger sister, the girl who had cried so loudly. As an afterthought, the teacher turned back toward her and asked, "Say, does she cry much at home? Is anything wrong?" The older sister looked away with a fixed smile, acting dumb. She shook her head and said nothing. The little girl didn't say anything either. There was no communication whatsoever, and after a while the sisters went away together. Curious, I followed them. Right outside the classroom door, the older sister asked the child what had happened. Very volubly, the little girl explained that "the teacher say she don' care if I cry!" "She say that, did she!" exclaimed the older sister with genuine concern. They talked animatedly together—two normal, intelligent, responsible little girls.

Now I know, I thought—now I know how to give these children a good head start in hating school.

Sign on the school wall: "F . . . all the whoa in this school." At P.S. 111, in the Hell's Kitchen neighborhood of New York, the children were Puerto Rican, Negro, Chinese. Some in the afternoon group, I was told, just made it to school after breakfast, at 1:00 P.M., having been out on the street all night with their parents, who liked to take the record player outside and dance. To accommodate them, only juice was served when they arrived; the hot lunch was served a little later.

"There's no question in my mind it's been very, very worth while," said Supervisor Harold Glasser about the summer program, now nearing its end. "With one adult for every five children, we could give them intensive individual attention.

"One child was found to have worms, and after seeing him the clinic suggested checking other members of his family too. It turned out that his mother was also ill—if she had had no treatment, she would have died within six months. She's fine now.

"Perhaps the best part is the involvement of parents. We run English classes for parents, and a sewing group in which they get instruction as well as the use of two machines. As a result, they now bring their problems to the parent coordinator, a local volunteer. School has become a warm place for people to live in—not just a place of authority that sends in bad reports about one's child."

His only criticism concerned the mountains of paper work required by Head Start. The Preschool Inventory test was too lengthy, he said, too late (it arrived in the fifth week, instead of the first), and it posed questions that were inappropriate for these children. For example, "How many broken arms do you have?"—intended to bring out the reply "None," but a very threatening question for children accustomed to many forms of violence. The Inventory had to be given to every third child in the program at the beginning and end of the summer to see how much progress had been made, but "We couldn't do the second series, as we only finished the first in the eighth week!"

The Head Start children's replies to the Inventory questions were revealing. To the question "What does a father do?" they gave answers like "He beats you up" or "He goes away." Few knew what a mother does; most of the time they did not answer that question. But they did know what a doctor does ("He sticks you") and what a policeman does ("He kills people").

It was the last week of Head Start at P.S. 165, on the edge of Harlem. A neat young teacher, who teaches kindergarten during the regular school year, was busy wrapping small presents for the children. To her enormous satisfaction, Head Start had provided the money for these treats—one of the program's nice touches—instead of her having to take the money out of her own pocket, as usual; in this kind of neighborhood, she explained, you couldn't ask parents to contribute anything.

"I think it's phenomenal how much they've grown," she said, glancing at the fifteen children in her group as they worked contentedly on some cutting and pasting, with help from the assistant teacher. "They're well trained for school. It's not difficult to keep order. They know what paint is, what clay is. I'd like to have them in my kindergarten class now."

The supervisor for the Head Start centers in this area, Irving Bernstein, said the summer experience had shaken him. It had made him take a fresh look at regular kindergarten classes, as well as at all the early grades.

"Those classes shouldn't have twenty-five children, but at most fifteen!" he declared. "Maybe it would be better to have thirty or thirty-five children to a class, if necessary; but then have two teachers, and also some volunteers. In kindergarten, many of these children are very, very quiet. They just come in and sit, and the teachers are so busy they pay little attention to them. The volunteers could at least talk to them, draw them out, allow them to speak." He also felt that parents should be brought into the school—and that to encourage them the school should provide baby sitters, or a rumpus room where small children could play. During the summer he had arranged for the local public library to run special storytelling hours for Head

Start children and their parents. The librarian showed parents how to read to children, explaining that they could take out children's books in both English and Spanish. "You'd be surprised how many parents didn't know that library facilities are free," he said.

In many areas, Head Start was swamped by applicants who came close to being middle-class, whereas the really poor either did not know about it or did not care. The most conscientious administrators, therefore, sent out people to beat the bushes for needy children, rather than just wait for them. Thus the White Plains, New York, school system employed a part-time nurse and a Negro school counselor specifically to visit families in poor neighborhoods and tell them about Project Head Start. "After this door-to-door contact, very few parents turned us down," said John Whritner, director of the White Plains program.

The mothers of Head Start children in his area were given a chance to meet with a social worker from time to time to discuss their problems. I attended one such meeting in the basement of a housing project, where two of the classes were held.

A plump woman spoke up first. "I don't want to knock Head Start," she began. "After all, my son's in there." (She was referring to an older boy, who worked as a paid aide; she also had a preschool child in the program.) "But we need really good teachers, experienced teachers who don't play around—who're not afraid of children, but make 'em *do* things. They should teach them letters—to *read*." Many of the other mothers nodded and seemed to agree with her.

This was not the attitude of the teachers, however. The head teacher tried to run a conventional nursery school, with a little more individual attention and more emphasis on language development. Her main goal was to make sure each child was given the experience of success at something, sometime during the day. The other teacher, a middle-aged graduate of Columbia Teachers College who had spent the past twenty years teaching future teachers how to teach, emphasized good manners: "Shake hands and look at me," she told each child in turn at the end of the day. "This is your book. Carry it this way. See you tomorrow!"

The books she referred to consisted of the children's own drawings and other work, put together by the teachers. Entitled "My Book," they bore an odd resemblance to the Preschool Inventory, one of the tests which were supposed to measure Head Start's effectiveness. "Head Start wants them to be able to draw squares, circles, and triangles," explained the teacher, showing me the squares, circles and triangles a child had drawn in his book. She meant no harm. On several other occasions, I saw teachers deliberately teach the items on this test for lack of any other curriculum.

One of the volunteers, an attractive college girl, complained that she had never been given any orientation about her duties. "I had never worked with children before," she said. "I came without any experience at all. We were told we'd be able to watch at first, but there was so much to do that we had to work right from the start. We were told there'd be in-service training, but it never materialized.

"I was supposed to take the children one by one and teach them shapes. But I hadn't the foggiest idea of how to begin teaching them shapes. I drew a square and asked them what it was, and they said, 'It's a window'!"

Even the regular teachers in Head Start centers received only six days of training before the program started. "We didn't have time to breathe," recalled Mr. Whritner. "It was just a case of getting it off the boards as quickly as possible." Despite all the rush and the paper work, which arrived by the ton, he felt the program had been very successful—if only in increasing the children's ability to sit still and follow instructions.

"The first day, the teachers could only take one or two children at a time for each activity," Mr. Whritner said. "Halfway through the program, pasting work could be done by two-thirds of the children—thirteen children—at one time." Though this was the very opposite of the individual attention for which Head Start makes so many claims, Mr. Whritner said it showed that the children had learned what was expected of them in a school setting. He might have added, "They're in the Army now."

HARYOU-ACT, the controversial Harlem community-action agency, had organized Head Start centers for 504 children. During the last week of the summer program, I visited a HARYOU center in one of the oldest school buildings in New York, P.S. 184. The school had a small, skimpy yard facing the street—its sole playground—with broken glass on the ground and many tall young men lounging about. Occasional baseball games went on there, as it was the only place available and open to anyone. Along one side of this small yard the Head Start children were taken out in small groups to sit in a row, play singing games, and drink their juice in the sun.

The head teacher was in the hospital, critically ill. In her absence, the class was run by an assistant teacher, a young Negro who was a senior in college. He had no trouble keeping the group under control, since the children were obviously delighted to have him around. He played wild games with them, romping about and letting them climb on him. "I play with them as I do with my younger cousins," he explained.

As to curriculum, he did pretty much what he pleased. "I don't want to knock Head Start," he said, echoing the mother in White Plains, "but we had no equipment at all in the first two weeks. Now, I know teachers are supposed to be creative—

but I'd never had experience with children *that* young!" On
his own, he decided to teach the children the alphabet. He made
a large felt board, on which felt-backed capital letters could be
stuck. Every day he asked the children whether they knew the
names of the letters he put up on the board. Those who knew
the answer were allowed to come up and feel the letters. He
also encouraged the children to paint letters during their painting sessions, rather than just do blobs.

He gave the children the Preschool Inventory test early in
the summer, and then—"I sort of used it as a guideline," he said
candidly. "It showed up what they didn't know, so I tried to
teach them that: to draw circles and squares, and know parts
of the body."

Some of the children in his group were only three, although
their parents had said they were four and a half; the truth didn't
come out until a few weeks later, by which time it seemed point-
less to object. Others were six, but had never been to kindergarten or any other school. Actually, he said, they seemed to
have learned just as much *without* kindergarten—he couldn't tell
the difference. Then he added, genuinely puzzled, "How much
can you teach them earlier, anyway? What *can* they learn at
that age? I don't know enough about it."

In the Hotel Theresa—a decrepit, old-fashioned, rambling
hotel where Fidel Castro once plucked his own chicken—HARYOU-
ACT's offices could be reached only after a uniformed policeman
checked one's pass, given out at the reception desk downstairs.
Upstairs, the coordinator for Head Start centers, Elaine Danavall,
gulped down a cup of coffee in lieu of lunch as her phone
kept ringing.

"One of the purposes of Head Start was to have language
development," she said. "But most teachers have had no training for it, so it was not emphasized as much as it should have
been. Nor did these teachers realize the special need for such a

program. It was an impossible task! There was no training before, and no in-service training."

She explained that HARYOU-ACT was toying with the idea of shorter sessions, perhaps adding care from a motherly person in the afternoon, to give the teachers a chance to do a better job. "Youngsters do need supervised play during the day, but they also need learning experiences and a chance to develop skills," she said. "Yet so often the children don't even go to kindergarten, when there is one, because it is open only half a day. If parents go to work, they can leave their child with a neighbor who'll be home all day, but they can't expect the neighbor to take the child to school and bring him back as well. So we're still trying to solve that one."

Head Start thus acted as a catalyst throughout the nation—making many old problems visible, forcing people to seek new solutions. Teachers were brought face to face with poverty for the first time as they visited the children's homes. School administrators began to criticize the size and organization of their regular kindergarten and first grades. Psychologists discovered the need for specialists at the preschool level to do the preventive work which becomes impossible if, as generally happens, everything is postponed until the third grade. Parents began to view schoolteachers and principals as people who might conceivably be on their side. And the lack of adequate day care emerged as a major barrier to the children's development.

Each part of the country had its own reactions to the influx of Head Start people, ideas, and money. In Mississippi, for example, Head Start became a pawn in the civil-rights struggle. The segregated school system opened one set of centers for Negro children with regular teachers. The Child Development Group of Mississippi (CDGM), many of whose members were involved in civil rights, opened another set of centers with teachers chosen for their "lively and loving way with children," rather than their grammar. As parents and neighbors pitched in to clear the grounds, build the buildings, run the classes, and watch the children, these centers instilled a strong sense of pride in all who took part in them. But they were soon swept up in the political opposition to CDGM, and the Office of Economic Opportunity temporarily withdrew its funds.

Elsewhere, Head Start became a pawn in the struggle between the old-guard specialists in early-childhood education, who emphasized free play as the prime method of promoting the child's emotional and social development, and the newer advocates of cognitive learning. The old guard won hands down.

Heavily weighted with physicians and traditionalists, Head Start's Planning Committee did not include a single person who represented the truly cognitive approach to preschool education.

Head Start's director, Dr. Julius B. Richmond, is a distinguished pediatrician whose interest in Head Start stems from his pioneering work on children's early psychosocial development. He also heads the pediatrics department at the State University's Upstate Medical Center, Syracuse, New York. For him, Head Start was a labor of love. He worked superhuman hours to get the project off the ground. And he seemed puzzled by some of the educationalists.

"The toughest bureaucracy I've had to deal with here is not the government, but the professionals," he declared. "They think that when middle-class kids come out well, it's because of their wonderful programs. It may have nothing at all to do with their programs—it's just that middle-class kids get enough out of their general backgrounds to come out well." When he asked such professionals what basis they had for their conviction that preschool programs should not be more structured, they generally replied that it was experience. But if all their experience is with middle-class children, Dr. Richmond pointed out, they shouldn't generalize in this way.

At his suggestion Dr. Bettye M. Caldwell, a young psychologist who had been working with him in Syracuse, drew up an alternative version of the Daily Program booklet; the original one faithfully mirrored the daily activities of middle-class nursery schools. The Caldwell version at once stirred up such a storm of protest among the consultants, however, that it was not released to Head Start centers until two years later.

In a flood of letters and telegrams, filled with exclamation marks, the experts expressed their horror: "Appalling!" "Reminiscent of kindergarten program of more than 45 years ago." "Contradicts everything we've been doing and saying!"—"stereotyped"—"rigid"—"repellent." The most extraordinary comment came from one expert who wrote, "For some reason, I'd as soon see the distribution of atom bombs to Head Start centers as mass distribution of this material."

Though the Caldwell booklets were scarce, I was fortunate enough to get one. Instead of a guide to Prussian drills, as I had been led to expect, I read a modest manual, filled with specific suggestions on how to help children learn the most from every activity. A feeling of urgency permeated this version. Snack time, it was suggested, should also be story time, since even a restless and noisy child would listen quietly while eating. Free play should be cut to an absolute minimum, leaving more time for matching games (to sharpen observation), puzzles, structured art work (to learn shapes and practice drawing lines), individualized books, and counting games of varying intensity. About half the activities required one-to-one attention from the teacher, or at least one adult for every three or four children. The importance of making children speak was emphasized throughout. Though one might disagree with some of these suggestions on various grounds, they represented a serious attempt to teach children basic skills without which they could not be expected to benefit from school.

After this fiasco, Head Start apparently gave up further efforts in the cognitive direction. Dr. Richmond took comfort in the fact that the Head Start program was comprehensive—it did something about all aspects of the child's life. At the same time, Head Start exerted a potent force for change in kindergarten classes and throughout the educational system. "Some people concerned with budgets complain that we're shooting costs up," said Dr. Richmond. "After all, the public schools spend only $500 per child per year. I just keep saying, You shouldn't be working with groups that large! We're an affluent country. And with only $500 a year, you get what you pay for."

His main concern, of course, was spreading education downward—toward children of three and four. Theoretically, Head Start was committed to this. In August, 1965, at the end of the first summer's program, President Johnson had announced that because of its success Head Start would be placed on a year-round basis. This would involve new, year-round centers for some 350,000 young children right away, and many more within the next five years. There would also be follow-through programs for children who had had the summer Head Start, and a repetition of the summer project itself.

Unfortunately, what could be conjured up on a crash basis in the summer, when schools were empty and teachers free, proved almost impossible to reproduce in winter. The plan at once ran into three difficulties: lack of space that local health departments would approve for young children; lack of teachers; lack of money.

A year-round program is obviously far more expensive than an eight-week summer program. The summer Head Start had cost roughly $170 per child, or a total of $84 million the first year, with OEO bearing 90 percent of the cost and local agencies paying the rest. By contrast, year-round classes cost about $1,000 per child. Providing such classes for the 350,000 children mentioned by President Johnson would require an additional $350 million per year.

Less than half the promised number of "full-year" classes appeared during the first year—and they were full-year in name only, averaging no more than four and a half months. Children of five and over still made up 42 percent of these classes. The number of younger children increased but slightly in 1966–67.

Meanwhile, nobody seemed to be giving much thought to what would be taught in the new classes for three- and four-year-olds, if they were ever started on a large scale. Their curriculum could not be the same as that of five- and six-year-olds in the summer program—yet no guidelines were being planned to spell out these differences. Nor were any provisions made for comparing the progress of children in various types of classes.

Similarly unguided, haphazard preschool education of poor children has usually proved academically useless in the past— especially when the experimenters were careful enough to compare the children in their programs with those whom they left out. Indianapolis offers an instructive example: Just before Head Start began, a highly regarded settlement house called Flanner House tried a preschool enrichment program for four-year-olds there. Nobody dreamed of questioning the belief that the program would work, at least to some extent. The idea was just to demonstrate how much good it could do. As scientifically as possible, thirty slum children were divided into two equal groups, matched for age, IQ, and general readiness. One group attended a play-oriented nursery school three times a week for seven months. The other group stayed home. At the end of the program, both groups were retested. To their dismay, the experimenters found no significant difference between the two groups as to intelligence, general information, or verbal ability. They tested the children again a year and a half later, when they were in first grade—and again found no difference between the group that had had the "enrichment" and the controls. Neither the Metropolitan Readiness Test nor ratings by their teachers enabled them to tell the children apart. Dr. Gerald D. Alpern, director of research in child psychiatry at the Indiana University Medical School, concluded that the experience of preschool attendance per se will not necessarily provide culturally disadvantaged children with an educational head start over those who don't attend.

Though Head Start turned its back on such developments, fruitful research was emerging from the nation's laboratories.

Chapter 3

THE NEW MIND-BUILDERS

Accoʀᴅɪɴɢ to the cognitive psychologists, an individual's achievement in life depends very largely on what he has been helped to learn before the age of four. If this startling theory is correct, it requires a radical change in society's approach to the years before a child enters school. It implies reversing the present pattern, in which we spend the bulk of our educational resources on more advanced students, and concentrating instead on children during their earliest years.

Such a change would be welcomed by the cognitive psychologists, who study the process of knowing. They are men obsessed with the passing of time and the irreparable damage now being done to millions of youngsters. With heroes of their own— among them Switzerland's eminent Jean Piaget, J. McV. Hunt, of the University of Illinois, and Harvard's Jerome S. Bruner— they hope to start a revolution of similar scope to that begun by Freud when he recognized the depth of children's earliest emotions, and their nearly indelible effects. The new mind-builders realize that children's earliest thoughts can have consequences as profound as those of their feelings.

The child's intelligence grows as much during his first four years of life as it will grow in the next thirteen, they point out. At two or three years of age, he can learn any language, perhaps even several languages, more easily than any adult. During this period of extra-rapid growth, the environment exerts its most powerful effect.

The cognitive psychologists assume that children who are deprived of early intellectual stimulation will never reach the heights of which they might be capable. For middle-class children, this may mean a loss of brilliance, a blunted and less interesting life, a smaller contribution to society—but, on the whole, they will make out all right. Middle-class homes usually provide a fairly varied and abstract environment for their youngest offspring, even without special planning; furthermore, middle-class parents tend to reward both curiosity and achievement.

For the children of poverty, however, an unplanned intellectual diet in the early years brings almost certain disaster—preordained failure in school and in adult life. The new mind-builders offer the first logical explanation for these children's intellectual handicap. They also offer some tentative methods of prevention before the age of four, and treatment thereafter.

Only the outer limits of a person's intelligence are fixed at birth, they believe. A given individual "may have an IQ of 80 with a poor environment, or 120 with a good environment," declares Illinois University's Samuel A. Kirk, an authority on special education. This is a breath-taking range: its bottom score places a person barely above the moron level, whereas the top score is typical of college graduates.

More conservative psychologists, such as Benjamin S. Bloom, of the University of Chicago, base their estimates on studies of identical twins who were separated at birth, and conclude that the environment's share is roughly 20 points of IQ—still a formidable span, which, says Bloom, could mean the difference between a life in an institution for the feeble-minded or a productive life in society. It could mean the difference between a professional career and an occupation which is at the semiskilled or unskilled level.

A scholarly, middle-aged man, Bloom does not make statements lightly. He is past-president of the American Educational Research Association. He is a meticulous researcher. Yet his book *Stability and Change in Human Characteristics*, published in 1964, provides the most powerful statistical ammunition for the new school of thought. Before writing it, Bloom pored over more than a thousand different studies of youngsters, each of which followed up certain children and measured them at various points in their development. Although made by different people over the past half-century, these studies showed such close agreement that Bloom began to see specific laws of development emerging, rather than mere trends.

For each human trait, Bloom found, there is a characteristic growth curve. Half of a child's future height, for example, is reached by the age of two and a half. Half of a male's aggressiveness is established by the age of three. Half of a person's "intellectuality," as well as general intelligence, is formed by the age of four. By the age of six, when a child enters school, he has developed as much as two-thirds of the intelligence he will have at maturity. Even with regard to purely academic achievement, at least one-third of the development at age eighteen has taken place prior to a child's entrance into the first grade at school.

Here is the first law that Bloom derives from his evidence: The environment will have maximum impact on a specific trait during that trait's period of most rapid growth. As an extreme example, a starvation diet would not affect the height of an eighteen-year-old, but could severely retard the growth of a one-year-old baby; furthermore, the loss of growth during the earliest period could never be fully made up.

As time goes on, Bloom believes, more and more powerful forces are required to produce a given amount of change in a child's intelligence—if it can be produced at all—and the emotional cost it exacts is increasingly severe.

In many ways, these are subversive theories. They tend to make people uncomfortable. Although most Americans accept the view that man's character is formed during his earliest years, the idea that man's intelligence is shaped at the same time seems alien, and very much harder to assimilate. It raises too many questions about the responsibility of home and society, as well as about the role of the school. It also conflicts with the popular notion that a child's main tasks during the early years are learning to get along with others and learning to adjust to the group.

Until the early 1960's—and in many quarters still today—the motto of right-thinking educators and parents was "Don't push" young children intellectually. Intelligence was supposed to be fixed at birth. Only emotional factors could tamper with its automatic development. Thus, deliberate stimulation or guidance of the intellect during the earliest years was either useless or harmful. The home was seen in terms of the emotional support it offered—not in terms of its "hidden curriculum."

The new cognitive psychologists, on the other hand, emphasize the eagerness with which children teach themselves skills when the environment is favorable. In their view, the youngest child feels a passionate urge to make sense of the world—to find out its rules and logic. Toddlers and infants are the most original scientists, the cleverest linguists—in fact, the most intellectually alert of all human beings, they declare. Unfortunately, adults often stifle these talents instead of developing them.

The mind-builders point to the torrent of questions that gush from the two-year-old as he learns to speak, or to the frenzy of the child who tries to walk by himself: Breathless with excitement, he propels himself forward as one holds his hand, screaming when one puts him down, scrambling to get up and try it again, ready to go on all day until he drops from fatigue. This is the zest for life and learning which they want to tap. They believe that a child who is given maximum opportunities to grow intellectually will also grow in self-confidence, and thus have a healthier emotional development than one kept too long in a gilded play-pen. Therefore they want to provide deliberate stimulation of the child's intellect almost from the moment of birth.

The mind-builders see the difference between babies from middle-class homes and those who are born into poverty emerging vividly about the age of one and a half. Until then, standard tests show most normal babies performing in pretty similar fashion; in some respects, such as motor development, the poorer-class infants even seem slightly ahead. But around the age of eighteen months, when babies begin to talk and generally throw their weight around—when they move from the physical to the cultural environment—their curves of development take widely divergent forms. The middle-class toddlers forge ahead, investigating their exciting world of toys, speech, and games under the guidance of interested adults. The children of poverty, in their crowded and disorganized homes, learn that the best way to stay out of trouble is to keep quiet. Whether they are cared for by an older sister, by an indifferent neighbor, or by their own exhausted and harried parents, the law is the same: Curiosity is generally rewarded by a whipping. Coincidentally, their IQ's begin to drop.

For children in this group, there are no nursery schools. Despite all the talk about Head Start and the importance of preschool education, only 6 percent of the nation's three-year-olds attend any nursery school—and these are mostly private schools for middle-class youngsters. Of the nation's four-year-olds, only 19 percent attend nursery schools—again, mostly private ones for middle-class children. Even at the kindergarten level, there are barely enough classes for 60 percent of the nation's five-year-olds.

By kindergarten age, however, these children have been so starved intellectually that their IQ's run some 5 to 15 points below those of their middle-class peers. The IQ's of children who don't enter school until the first grade tend to be even lower, illustrating what some investigators have called a "cumulative deficit."

With every year in school, the IQ's of slum children continue to sink, until they reach a level some 20 points below that of more privileged children. Since the IQ is a comparative figure, based on how the majority of other children of the same age are doing, this does not mean that they have become more stupid than before, but it does mean that they have failed to grow intellectually while middle-class children did. Thus the gap between the classes widens, and whatever promise, talent, or genius the slum child may have had potentially is effectively squelched.

"First the child is expected to learn in a competitive situation with more advantaged children, which leads to a decline in his confidence and his self-image," says Professor Bloom, "then we incarcerate him for a ten-year period in a place where all the cards are stacked against him." As Bloom sees it, the effect of cultural deprivation is the same throughout the world, punishing Negroes, Puerto Ricans, working-class Englishmen, and Yemenites with equal ferocity. Unless special measures are taken in the early years, the schools soon become breeding places for emotional decline or disturbances in children from all these groups.

If a child's educational achievements depend so heavily on what he learned before the age of six, the home—not the school —emerges as the major educational institution in the land. Thus, researchers have begun to compare the hidden curriculum in various types of homes. They are finding some exceptions in every social group—families whose children consistently do well or fail, despite all statistical probability—and they are trying to isolate what caused them.

This naturally leads to the question, What should be done when the home fails? Should one just sit back and watch millions of children march toward wholesale school failure, or should one intervene? Bloom makes it clear that a brief crash program, such as the summer Head Start, is not likely to produce lasting effects. At what age, then, should one begin—and how long should the intervention go on? What, exactly, do children learn during their earliest years?

Enter the hero of the cognitive psychologists: the world-renowned Swiss professor Jean Piaget, now seventy years old, whose monumental work on children's mental growth was generally ignored in the United States until an English translation of one of his major books appeared in 1952, found sympathetic readers, and sparked a Piaget boom which is still in full swing.

What Freud had done for the emotions, Piaget did for the intellect. He charted man's intellectual growth in such bold strokes, backed by such minute detail, that people who study him can never see the subject in the same light again. As with Freud, Piaget's brilliant analysis of how children develop runs the risk of being popularized into a mere parlor game. Whenever a book or article appears about some facet of Piaget's experiments with children—really not experiments at all, but stage settings for extremely pointed and accurate observations—hundreds of parents start trying out the same experiments on their own children.

Most popular now are Piaget-inspired "conservation" experiments—attempts to find out whether a preschool child can "conserve," that is, understand that changes in shape do not affect quantity. Surprisingly, four-year-olds usually believe that there is more juice in a small glass that is filled to the brim than in a large glass that is only half-full—even when they see it being poured back and forth. They also believe that they have more cracker when it is broken up into several pieces, and that a lump of Play-dough becomes bigger or smaller according to its shape. Only the simplest equipment is required to set the stage for a variety of delightful conservation experiments that can give some clues to the child's level of reasoning. But their true significance becomes clear when one looks at Piaget's work as a whole.

While Freud based his major theories on an analysis of himself, Piaget's most original theories come from an extraordinarily detailed, systematic, and creative observation of his own three children.

Laurent, Lucienne, and Jacqueline Piaget were undoubtedly the world's best-observed babies, with Papa carrying the notion of the "baby book" to unmatched heights. Beginning with Observation 1 ("From birth sucking-like movements may be observed . . .") and other details which Piaget believes are as theoretically important as they are factually trite, he traces the way in which the child adapts and organizes his behavior. At first the newborn sucks whatever happens to rub his lips—his own hand, a quilt, or Papa's index finger. But by the twentieth day of life, Laurent stops sucking objects that produce no milk, cries, and actively gropes with his mouth for the nipple. Piaget terms this shift from a passive response to active groping an example of both assimilation—the inner organization of information—and accommodation—the modification of existing patterns to conform with outer reality.

At the age of three months and five days, Lucienne shows the first signs of "intention," of deliberately trying to make something interesting go on. Papa had hung some cloth dolls over her bassinet, and Lucienne discovered that when she kicked her legs, the bassinet shook, making the dolls swing from the hood. "Lucienne looks at them, smiling, and recommences at once," writes Piaget in Observation 94. When he places the dolls at different heights, she learns to reach them with her foot and shake them.

This interest in prolonging or repeating certain sights and sounds is what makes the baby learn new skills, Piaget points out. He learns to throw objects, pick them up, rattle them, reach them with or without tools, find them when they have disappeared—and discovers that objects have properties of their own. Here lie the origins of children's curiosity, and much depends on the fate of these earliest efforts.

The first glimmerings of intelligence occur as the child gropes his way to new methods—for example, finding that he can get Papa's watch by pulling the pillow it rests on. The broader the child's repertoire—a function of experience—the more new means of this sort he can discover.

Genuine intelligence, in Piaget's terms, emerges just a little later, toward the end of what he calls the sensorimotor period —the period of development that lasts from birth to one-and-one-half or two years of age. At the end of this period, Piaget's children begin to invent new methods through mental combination, rather than through groping. It is the take-off point for abstract thought.

To illustrate this new power of invention, which Piaget calls the most delicate problem that any theory of intelligence has to treat, he tells how his son Laurent, at sixteen months and five days, all at once discovered the use of a stick as a tool. Jacqueline and Lucienne had come to similar discoveries after long and repeated practice playing with sticks. Laurent, on the other hand, "looks at the bread, without moving, looks very briefly at the stick, then suddenly grasps it and directs it toward the bread. . . ." An hour later, Papa tries putting a toy just out of reach of Laurent, and a new stick next to him. Sure enough, Laurent does not even try to catch the object with his hand; he immediately grasps the stick and draws the toy to him.

Piaget seems fascinated with this leap into abstraction. It reminds him of the freedom gained by older children as they stop having to count with their fingers to establish that two plus two make four, and simply combine the numbers. Each feat required a variety of previous experiences, he points out, as well as a repertoire of images with which the child could visualize certain sequences of cause and effect.

During the important preconceptual phase, which follows the sensorimotor period and lasts roughly until the age of four, the child constructs symbols and learns language. It is a time of much make-believe. It is also the What's that? stage, so well known to parents. As Piaget interprets this question, it indicates not just a wish to know the names of things, but a wish to understand what class of things each one belongs to. It is the beginning of "classification," a key element in the child's acquisition of logic. (For example, at two years three months of age, my youngest son noticed the moon for the first time and classified it as "ball!") At this stage, the logic often escapes adults, since it is based on the child's private—and frequently inaccurate—generalizations.

When Lucienne was thirty-eight months and twenty days old, writes Piaget, they passed a man, and Lucienne asked, "Is that man a daddy?" Piaget replied with the question "What is a daddy?" Lucienne answered, "It's a man. He has lots of Luciennes and lots of Jacquelines." "What are Luciennes?" asked Piaget. "They're little girls and Jacquelines are big girls." At this point, Piaget commented, the child was still reasoning without genuine concepts, "without the reversible nestings of a hierarchy of classes and relations."

Any parent can add his own illustrations of such private misconceptions, of the fanciful explanations three-year-olds have for everything around them, from firemen ("They repair the smoke") to the rain ("It washes the streets").

The next phase, which Piaget calls the intuitive phase, lasts from age four to seven or eight. This is the time of the famous conservation experiments. Although the child of two knows that objects exist even when they are hidden under a pillow, the child of four has not yet learned that a quantity of liquid remains the same regardless of the container into which it is poured. His attention is centered on some particular aspect of the containers—their number, their size, or how full they are. He cannot yet think of reversing the pourings; nor can he understand what a reversal would imply. The younger the child, the less reversible his thought. And without full "reversibility," there can be no conservation of quantity, which Piaget sees as a major landmark, occurring somewhere around the age of seven or eight, but sometimes earlier or later.

The more new things a child has seen and heard, the more he wants to see and hear—this seems to be Piaget's motto. The greater variety of things a child has coped with, the greater his capacity for coping. Thus, both curiosity and rate of intellectual development are tied to the variety of situations that have forced the child to modify previous patterns of thought. Each child writes his own intellectual history. The environment matters not so much for its own qualities as for the elements to which the child pays attention—and these vary with what he has previously assimilated. Piaget adds that there is pleasure in new accommodations and assimilations, as evidenced by the common urge to repeat new patterns that are almost, but not quite, learned.

It is a dynamic view, this picture of the child's intelligence as a continuously shifting adaptation to the environment—and completely at odds with popular notions. In his well-known book

The First Five Years of Life, a favorite with American parents, Arnold Gesell described stages of development as if they depended on a built-in time clock that would make them unfold automatically. Maturation, he implied, will take care of everything—just wait! Piaget gives maturation of the central nervous system its due—"it simply opens up possibilities"—but adds that it "never is sufficient in itself to actualize these possibilities. This actualization requires the child's use of the new form, as well as the influence of both the physical and the social environment."

Such is the worship of Piaget these days that when the great man recently flew to Philadelphia for a single lecture, thousands flocked to see him in the flesh. It was a memorable occasion. With his fringe of long, straight white hair down the sides and back of his balding head, his high forehead, horn-rimmed glasses, gold watch chain, and well-worn leather briefcase, he looked like a stock character—The Professor. On the platform, he commanded instant respect. Speaking in a booming voice, in French, he began by describing some of the key stages of children's intellectual development. Then he said, "The first question which I am always asked in the United States is, can one accelerate these stages?" (Laughter in the audience.) By way of reply Piaget pointed out that though all children must go through the sensorimotor period before learning to speak, they learn to speak at various ages. The fact that stages occur in the same sequence does not imply that they must always occur at the same chronological age. Quite substantial differences can be seen, particularly in different social milieus. Therefore Piaget's answer to the American question is, One *can* accelerate these stages, but not indefinitely—and there is not much to be gained by doing it beyond a certain measure.

Piaget thus emerged as a very reluctant hero, from the standpoint of those who would develop children's talents to the utmost by special intervention during the earliest years. In a sense, he disowned much of what was being done in his name. His own interest lay in *describing* certain processes, rather than changing them. As he emphasized, he is a psychologist, not an educator. Yet while he discouraged extreme attempts at accelerating children's intellectual development, he agreed that children in intellectually stimulating environments advanced more rapidly than others. His theories also explained why environments that restrict children's opportunities to explore, to test their own hypotheses, to have their questions answered and other questions raised, would retard their development.

A much more willing hero, Piaget implied, was Jerome S. Bruner, of Harvard, author of the famous dictum that "any subject can be taught effectively in some intellectually honest form to any child at any stage of development." That statement, said Piaget, "has always filled me with the deepest wonderment." It would take a grown woman three years to learn the theory of relativity—how long would it take a two-year-old? There is an optimal speed of learning, at which learning is most effective, he continued; but this is still very poorly understood. The real problem for schools is not to decide *what* should be taught, but *why*—what learning is really for. "Is the purpose to know a certain number of things, or is it to become capable of creating, of inventing new things?" Piaget asked.

The best way to facilitate a child's transition from one stage of intellectual development to the next is to let the student re-invent by himself whatever we want him to attain, he declared. But this makes the teacher's role much more difficult. He must then (1) set problems—the child also does this by himself, but the teacher can prepare the materials, or create appropriate situations; and (2) offer conflicting evidence when the child is too quickly satisfied with his solutions, so as to introduce a temporary lack of equilibrium that will force him to modify previously assimilated patterns of thought.

The day after his lecture, Piaget flew back to Geneva, where he is professor of psychology and codirector of the Institute of Educational Sciences. At Kennedy International Airport, between planes, he gave me a brief interview and a bit of advice: "Go see Bruner," he said. "He is an optimist."

There is considerable rivalry between Piaget's group, which pioneered in studies of children's intellectual development, and its nearest American equivalent, the Harvard Center for Cognitive Studies, which was established in 1960. On the eleventh floor of a modern, white building that looms over the rest of Harvard—the new William James Hall for the Behavioral Sciences—Professor Jerome S. Bruner, director of the Center, paced back and forth as he talked.

"Piaget has given us our richest picture of cognitive development—but he has never tried either to deprive a child of stimulation, or to enrich a child's environment, or even to teach," he declared, speaking volubly. He was wearing round, steel-rimmed glasses with thick lenses that made his eyes appear abnormally large, dominating his face. "I cannot believe that, just by happenstance, we have the optimum technique for bringing man to his optimum potential. Our present techniques of education go back to the time when we were still sitting on a rock."

I said Piaget had told me to come see him "because you are an optimist about how much can be taught young children."

"Optimist, pessimist—I'm just a pragmatist!" Bruner exclaimed, waving his arms for emphasis. "I have been urging that the growth of mind is very strongly dependent on the kinds of tools one uses. Man is born in a virtually naked state, helpless. If you take a look at the movement forward from monkeys to apes, from chimpanzees to man, you will find less and less specialized everything else and more specialized associative areas in the brain. Evolution seems to have favored creatures that were born less well developed, closer to the fetus. Man's development depends on three kinds of tool systems: for manipulating, for looking, and for symbolization. I cannot conceive of growth just from the inside out. Man is born naked, and culture shapes him.

"Piaget is a former zoologist—he used to study mollusks—and he describes ideal forms. I take a much more pragmatic view: The innate machinery in man never realizes its potential unless it's *linked to something*. The human language is a dynamo—it's capable of putting the world upside down—but it's only used as a doorbell marker, for labels!

"If by the age of fifteen a young man has a powerful set of tools, think where he'll be when he is twenty! We are only now on the threshold of knowing the range of educability of man—the perfectibility of man. We have never addressed ourselves to this problem before."

According to Bruner, this decade will see the birth of a new field, to be called the growth sciences. It will include all the specialties that deal with human growth, from education to anthropology and linguistics; it will also use "those young hotshot electronic characters" who are doing new kinds of experiments with the aid of computers. Bruner himself, a psychologist, is conducting computer-aided research on how newborns learn to correlate different perceptions; at the time of my visit, he was busy installing in Massachusetts General Hospital electronic equipment for this purpose. An extremely influential man, who is involved in nearly all aspects of education, he remains most concerned with how children develop their systems of processing information.

There are three ways in which the young go about things, deal with information in the world, he says. Describing an experiment with a board on which electric bulbs could be set to light up in any one of three patterns, he tells how children of various ages reacted when they were asked to find out which pattern was represented. "The four-year-old presses all over the board, and hardly ever solves the problem," says Bruner; "he's in a state of glee when he presses three things in a row and something lights up. At five, a child will check each of the images at once. But only at seven or eight will a child begin to combine these images into an information space, and use the rules of overlap, inclusion, exclusion. He'll stop for a minute, press one bulb, and know that if it doesn't go on, it can only be the third pattern. So, action first; imagery second; symbols third."

Accordingly, Bruner believes, the main job of preschools should be to work toward the translatability of one into the other: actions into pictures and speech. Growth takes place entirely when we recognize discrepancies between systems.

In his opinion, most of today's nursery schools are extremely old-fashioned in their emphasis on the process of expressing inner life. We have erred in overexpressing without constraint or art, he declares. The great question now is *not* the question of expression, but of how to prepare the child to bring some artistry into whatever he is doing. To produce problems we can work on and solve, we tend generally to turn our troubles into puzzles. The process of education is giving a person a stock of puzzle forms to impose on uncertainties.

The Center studies only human beings, whether children or adults. As someone noted with pride, there is not one rat maze or one grain of pigeon food on the premises. This represents a new direction for American psychologists, many of whom have distinguished themselves either for their work with animals, or for work that might just as well have been done with animals —studies of overt and observable behavior, rather than of the processes underlying it. Until recently, for example, few American scholars were working on the learning process itself.

The Center's opening in 1960 was only one sign of the times.

Shortly afterward, the bible of the new cognitive psychologists appeared: a revolutionary book, entitled *Intelligence and Experience*, by a professor of psychology at the University of Illinois, J. McV. Hunt. Almost overnight this weighty tome became a best-seller. In it, Hunt sounds the call to arms with his conclusion: "It is reasonable to hope to find ways of raising the level of intellectual capacity in a majority of the population. . . . It is one of the major challenges of our time."

Hunt believes that future generations of human beings can become far more intelligent—gaining an average of perhaps 30 IQ points—through better management of young children's encounters with their environment. The crucial problem is what he calls "the problem of the match"—finding the most stimulating circumstances for each child at each point in his development. Given anything too incongruous, children will withdraw, or ignore it; anything too familiar, and they will have no need to modify existing patterns of thought. The trick is to find circumstances with "an optimum of incongruity"—just a little beyond what the child has already stored in his brain.

When Myrtle McGraw, a famous woman psychologist of the 1930's, trained an eleven-month-old baby boy to roller-skate, that was a good match, says Hunt. The roller-skating lessons started when Johnny was just beginning to learn to walk, and "when a child is developing the walking schema, the addition of roller skates is only a relatively slight variation from the environmental situation he faces in getting up on his own two feet." Johnny roller-skated with skill by the time he was sixteen months old. On the other hand, his twin, Jimmy, who did not begin his lessons until he was twenty-two months of age, made no progress at all for a long time. Hunt notes that when skates were added to an already established walking schema, there was too much discrepancy between the feedback inputs from roller skating and those the child expected from walking. Therefore Jimmy had to overcome some emotional disturbances as well as to remake well-established patterns of motion.

This helps to explain why children learn foreign languages most easily at the same time they are learning to speak. Hunt points out that Piaget's stages could serve as clues to the kind of experiences a child would find most challenging. He also points out that a good match produces so much intrinsic motivation and pleasure that it becomes unnecessary to worry about pushing children.

Today's kindergartens, says Hunt, often provide a very poor match for middle-class children who have had two years of nursery school, because they offer too much of the same. They also provide a poor match for children from the slums, for opposite reasons. Only a few educators, such as Montessori, have found practical answers to the problem of the match on an individual basis, by letting each child select sequences at his own level.

With years of teaching behind him, Hunt feels sad about the large number of students who have trouble in college because, for the first time in their school lives, they're not told what to do, and yet their thirst for knowledge has never been developed. Others, raised very permissively, were free to do anything as children, but there was nothing they really wanted to do.

Hunt points out that Piaget's observations were all made when his children were comfortable and well fed. Various experiments have shown that satiated rats will explore things just for the fun of it, even if they have to suffer electric shocks to reach them. Satiated monkeys will solve intricate puzzles over and over again, for the joy of mastering them, and learn new tasks just for a chance to peek through a window at students walking by. There is a hierarchy of motivational systems, Hunt believes. Pain-avoidance dominates all others. Hunger, thirst, and other homeostatic needs come next, followed by sex, plans, and finally information-processing, which includes aesthetic experiences. The need for food can interfere with sex, and when one has a plan that is frustrated it dominates information-processing. When all four major systems are satisfied, however, information-processing comes into its own as a source of pleasure. Thus, if otherwise satisfied and provided with a good match, children will learn for the sake of learning; it will become a sport, as engrossing as tennis or baseball.

"My hunch is, we've never really tapped the potential of human beings," Hunt said, leaning back in his chair in his office at the University of Illinois's Psychological Development Laboratory. The early months and first couple of years are probably the most important, so the idea is to do this from birth on—to manage the child's life in a way that will maximize his *joie de vivre*, and keep him interested as he goes along.

Nevertheless, Hunt has two worries. "What I'm afraid of is that middle-class parents will use the new theories about intellectual development to keep up with the Joneses through their children—and withhold approval or affection unless the child performs," he says thoughtfully. "This would leave the child feeling worthless, with a drive to achievement for fear of failure, instead of intrinsic interest. This is a real danger."

He also fears that, in the first flush of enthusiasm about the idea that the bright can be made brighter, and children from the slums rescued from cycles of ignorance and poverty, the public will insist on utilizing what is not yet ready for uniform utilization. While the new mind-builders agree on the promise of the future, they disagree violently on how best to manage children's early environments today. This disagreement, says Hunt, shows that we're just ready to do research and development on the new techniques: We must try out what we think we know, but be prepared to change methods, if necessary, as we get evidence of what really fosters intellectual development and what does not. At present, he insists, the only thing he is confident about is that early experience *is* important, perhaps in ways we haven't even dreamed of.

Awareness of this importance is spreading. Even the usually conservative National Education Association has gone on record asking for free public schooling for all four-year-olds. The generally accepted school-starting age of six, it declared, is now obsolete. Despite the widespread lack of preparedness, public education for all children above the age of three seems around the corner. Dr. William Fowler, of Yeshiva University, New York, predicts that within a generation the world is destined to find itself caring for, and cognitively cultivating, its children from the cradle on. There is no evidence that guided stimulation has ever harmed young children, he says, but there is plenty of evidence that no human being of high ability has ever grown up without it.

As to *what* will be taught to young children, and *how*, this remains an open question, a fluid field, with competing philosophies jockeying for influence.

Chapter 4

THE PRESSURE-COOKER

APPROACH

THE "most horrible" of all the new programs for preschool children, according to some conservative teachers—the one that's really shaking up people in this field—is being run by two young men at the University of Illinois, in Urbana. So far, it has produced more rapid change in culturally disadvantaged four- and five-year-olds than any other technique can claim, at least in certain specific skills. But it is not a system for the fainthearted, nor for those with weak vocal chords.

In effect, Carl Bereiter and Siegfried Engelmann are operating an intellectual pressure cooker for children from the slums. They have totally rejected the standard, play-oriented nursery school, and make no attempt to reproduce a middle-class environment for these youngsters. Instead, they concentrate fiercely on a few areas, and drill the children like marines for two hours a day.

There were fifteen four-year-olds in the first class I visited, a few weeks after the opening of school. Three were newcomers being trained separately to catch up with the others. Their teacher was a rather loud, forceful, but not unpleasant woman with a Southern accent. "These are blocks," she said, showing some blocks, but hardly pausing for breath. "These are blocks. Say it all together—These are *blocks*. Now listen carefully. Are *these* blocks? Yes, these are blocks. What are these? Listen carefully. What are these?" A little Negro boy who had been listening as though hypnotized replied, "Blocks." "Give me the whole sentence," admonished the teacher. "These are blocks." Switching to a large ball, she went right on. "This ball is *big*," she said. "Say it all together now—This ball is *big*."

While one group practiced language, another group of four-year-olds worked on letters and a third learned arithmetic. Standing in front of a blackboard, their blonde teacher wrote, "$1 + 0 = 1$," and translated it for them, pointing as she spoke: "Start out with one, get no more—get zero more. One plus zero equal one. Say it for me." The children said it, then chanted in unison as she pointed to other equations on the board: "Two plus zero equal two, three plus zero equal three, four plus zero equal four," they sang out with great relish, clapping their hands rhythmically. Catching the youngsters' rollicking spirit, the teacher said, "Real loud now. Talk *big!*" "Eight plus zero equal *eight*," they screamed at the top of their lungs, obviously enjoying it. "$9 + 0 = ?$" wrote the teacher. "Nine plus zero equal *nine!*" yelled the children. "Good!" shouted the teacher, applauding them enthusiastically.

At first this seems only a noisy and rather unpleasant version of old-fashioned learning by rote. The children are steamrollered along, given no chance to slacken their pace or to withdraw from it all. Some of the newcomers seem bewildered. But the majority are very much with it, and they obviously enjoy the chance to make noise. It's an intensely physical kind of teaching: rhythmic movements, clapping of hands, cheers like those of a cheerleader, lots of concrete objects related to the matter at hand, arm and hand movements to illustrate points. The chants serve to remind the children how to proceed, attack problems, think.

"$1 + 1 = \square$," the teacher wrote on the board. Then each child came in turn to the blackboard, to point to and translate each symbol: "One plus one equal box." Then, together, all the children yelled (in rising hexameter): "Whenéver you sée a bóx, you háve to fígure-it-oút." The teacher said, "The problem tells you what to do: Start out with one (the children raise one finger), get more—one more! You end up with two! Count your fingers, one, two. So I can erase the box, and put in a two: $1 + 1 = 2$."

End of arithmetic class. The children are rewarded with hugs and with raisins "because you've all worked hard." The teacher has a special comment for each child; for instance, telling one in a friendly way that "you should speak up more, because I can't hear you!" No chance to teach is passed up. To get his raisins each child must answer the question, "Which is your right hand?" in the approved manner: "This is my right hand." To get his juice he must say, "My cup is blue," or whatever color his Dixie cup may be. The children relax as they drink and move around.

The ease with which children can be taught, first to parrot these rules, then to apply them, is somewhat frightening. An English visitor commented, "We'll have to be very careful whom we use as teachers—think what a totalitarian government could do with this!"

But the teachers themselves have no doubts—they are fully committed and enthusiastic. "You see us at the tooth-pulling stage," volunteers one of the teachers, an attractive middle-aged woman. "It's difficult at first, and there is some pressure, yes. But it's worth it because they're so happy when they're successful for the first times in their lives. They know when they're successful. We don't have to give them any tangible rewards like raisins after the first month. What we do is use language as a tool for figuring things out. We do systematically, and artificially, what middle-class parents do naturally at home. We started with ten-minute classes, but now we can go on for fifteen or twenty minutes at a time."

All the children now gather around the piano to sit on the floor for a period of singing. They are joined by Bereiter and Engelmann, the two iconoclasts who devised this program.

Bereiter, the project's director, holds a Ph.D. in educational psychology and a post as professor at the University of Illinois' Institute for Research on Exceptional Children. In his professional papers, as well as in his speech, he is refreshingly direct and clear—a man who knows his own mind. Now he sits at the piano. Looming over the seated children, he peers down at their faces, anxiously scanning them to see how much they understand. He hardly glances at the keyboard as he plays simple chords to the tune of "The Old Gray Mare, She Ain't What She Used to Be."

Ziggy Engelmann, his associate, leads the group with his booming voice. A few years ago he quit his vice-presidency in an advertising agency because he "just didn't feel it was worth while." Tall and muscular, he seems endowed with inexhaustible energy.

"Who remembers that *hard* word—vehicle?" he asks, seated among the children and emphasizing the word "hard" in the manner of a good comedian. There are shouts, "I do!" "What kind of vehicles do you know?" asks Engelmann. The children suggest bus, truck, and so on. "Let's sing it," says Engelmann, leading the group: "If it's a fire truck, it's a vehicle, it's a vehicle, it's a vehicle. . . ." He goes through all the vehicles the children suggest. "Now, who remembers what a weapon is?" A boy yells, "Gun—a spear." Engelmann leads the group again:

"If it's a rifle, then it's a wea-a-pon," and makes gestures showing a rifle being aimed. The children at once imitate him.

For a change of pace, Engelmann then sings, "Hey, everybody, touch your foot!" They do it, singing with him and laughing. "Touch your elbow, your knees—say knees, both of them! Touch both of them! Now listen"—and he speaks very delicately—"*one knee.*" Bereiter's intelligent face takes it all in. Most of the children do most of these things, but one newcomer, a pale little boy, small for his age, looks lost and turns his back on the whole thing. He stares ahead blankly, only occasionally repeating a syllable of the songs. The teacher who had worked with the newcomers' group sits next to him and tries to encourage him.

After the songs, Engelmann holds up a large board on which the alphabet is printed in capital letters. "Here we go now," he says. "You have to look up here." The children then sing the alphabet with him as he points to the letters.

The entire program lasts two hours each day—twenty minutes each for three different subjects, with interruptions for juice, drawing, writing, singing, and outdoor activities. "Our goal is to put these kids on an equal footing with more privileged kids when they enter school," Bereiter told me later. "It's not simply to produce improvement—any decently run preschool can do that. So we have to step up our pace. The middle-class child between four and five is learning, too, so these children have to learn a bit faster.

"We have virtually no free play—just the first ten minutes, and the singing, which is pretty structured. Free play is too time-consuming, and it is superfluous. 'Group experience,' 'playing with their peers,' are the *least* of these kids' needs. In some ways they're much less infantile than midde-class children. It's a rare middle-class child of four who can show genuine compassion; but with these kids, if you suddenly notice one of them is crying and you don't know why, ask the other children—they're aware, they know what's wrong. Many of these kids have served as baby sitters. They do a great deal of comforting each other."

The children look neat and well-dressed, some of them dressed much more carefully than middle-class children in a private nursery school. There is something touching about the great care and effort that must have gone into preparing them for school. About half of them are Negro, half white.

Bereiter explains that this year's group is very different, much less culturally deprived than last year's four-year-olds, who are now five and in a special kindergarten. This year's four-year-olds were selected from Aid to Dependent Children rolls and public-housing lists, in much the same way that children are selected for Head Start. "This proved to be a mistake as a means of recruiting," says Bereiter. "To get into public housing you must be a middle-class kind of person who just happens to have a low income; you need a letter of recommendation from your employers and other proof of respectability. Children on ADC rolls may or may not be culturally deprived—they may simply be poor because of their father's death or disability. Last year we used recommendations from teachers, who picked out the younger brothers and sisters of those children who seemed to need most help, and we ended up with an entirely different group—there were only two kids from a housing development, and all the children were Negro. There was only a one-third overlap with this year's bunch. We changed the procedure this year—though it was not my choice—because we had to have some *standard* for selection."

When last year's group came in, they could barely speak. Only two or three of them could say the simplest sentence. One child had been diagnosed as brain-damaged, for he just babbled and, according to Bereiter, was "a wild little kid." This year they all attend a special kindergarten, with teachers provided by Bereiter at the Hays School, a nearly all-Negro elementary school. When they enter Urbana's regular school system next year, they will be on their own. Since Urbana has a nongraded primary school, with twelve different tracks within the first three grades, the results should prove interesting.

At the Hays School kindergarten, I watched as the children wrote 2's on pieces of lined paper. Two teachers, both women, went from child to child to see how he or she was doing. As Engelmann walked into the classroom, he asked one little boy how many 2's he had written, and the child counted up to twenty. A teacher reported to Engelmann that two of the boys had misbehaved. Sternly, he told them to follow him, took them to another room and lectured them for a few minutes; they came out quietly and took their seats. Then the group split into three parts, with Engelmann taking over the top section for math: two boys and two girls.

"It's time to think about—*work!*" he began, fairly roaring. "Are you ready for tough stuff?" On the blackboard he wrote, "$8 + 3 = ?$" Immediately the children started to shout: "Eight plus zero equal eight, eight plus one equal nine, eight plus two equal ten, eight plus three equal eleven!" "Very good," shouted Engelmann. "Now let's see how tough you are." And he wrote, "$9 + 4 = ?$" Same reaction from the class, except that now they end up with a special flourish, drawing out the "thuh-uh-*uhr*-teen!" "Oh, she's tough!" exclaims Engelmann, pointing to the girl who had screamed loudest and fastest. "She's *tough!* But I'm really going to get you on the next one. I'll fool you! You'll be all washed up!" And he writes, "$15 + 3 = ?$" The children start to scream in the usual way, clapping their hands as they count. "You'll never get it!" shouts Engelmann, by way of encouragement. Two of them do get distracted this time and stop at seventeen. "Seventeen?" asks Engelmann. "No! I almost got you!" but the others go on to eighteen, shouting at the top of their lungs to drown out the error. As they scream, clap their hands, or roar with laughter, the noise is deafening.

"All right," Engelmann calls out, "who can read this?" The symbols on the blackboard begin to look like algebra: $15 + a = 18$. He leads the group, with rising inflection: "Fifteen plus *what* equals eighteen?" The answer is easy, since they just solved this a moment ago. Then Engelmann writes, "$7 - b = 2$," and lets the children go to work.

"Seven and b are not the same size," they shout, "because you're not ending up with zero. So—seven minus zero equal seven, seven minus one equal six, seven minus two equal five, seven minus three equal four, seven minus four equal three, seven minus five equal *two!*"

Next, Engelmann writes on the board, "$\Delta - 8 = 3$," reading it aloud, "Triangle minus eight equal three." Undismayed, the pupils shout, with occasional prodding from Engelmann, "Triangle and eight are not the same size, because you're not ending up with zero. So triangle is bigger than eight. It's three bigger than eight. What's three bigger than eight? What's one bigger than eight? Nine! What's two bigger than eight? Ten! What's three bigger than eight? Eleven! So *triangle is eleven!*" (triumphantly).

In the same room, adding to the noise, six other children face another blackboard and also yell replies to their teacher's questions. They shout out the days of the week and the seasons, stressing the key prepositions: "Spring is *after* winter." "Summer is *after* spring." "Is fall *before* summer?" asks the teacher. "No," the children shout. One little boy keeps rocking sideways on his chair as if to ease the tension of his efforts. "Fall is *after* summer!" he shouts, and then bursts out, "Me and Jimmy are doing a good job!"

This is the lowest track, intellectually. The subject being taught them during this period would have been called "language" the year before—it corresponds to the statements the four-year-old newcomers were repeating—but now the teachers call it "causality," for it includes bits of science and everyday knowledge presented so as to stress causal relationships. The teacher now draws a wide curve, like a horizon, on the blackboard, and tells the children this will be the earth. "What do you want me to put on it?" she asks. The answers are slow in coming, and she must remind the children more than once to pay attention, but finally they suggest a house, some people, the sun. "Where does the sun go?" she asks before sketching it. "Above or below the earth?"

In another classroom, I watched children from the middle-level section of the same kindergarten reading all together from a linguistic series. The title of the story is "Fat Nat." "Pat fat Nat on the mat," they read. Then they take turns, doing one line each: "Fat Nat is on a mat." "Pat Nat." "Nat sat on the mat." Not surprisingly, they seem unenthusiastic. The reading matter is even duller, though more logical in its selection of words, than standard Dick-and-Jane readers. They read haltingly and, for the first time in this program, do not shout—in fact, they speak quite low. According to the teacher, they read at about mid-first-grade level. The staff is not entirely satisfied with the books on hand, but believes there is little to choose from.

Back upstairs, the math group is still vociferous and active. Facing a large multiplication chart that has been placed beneath the blackboard, they work on fractions. Engelmann has written the equation $7/1 = b$ on the board. "What fraction does seven equal?" he asks. "Can you prove it for me?" Pointing to the multiplication chart, one child proves that seven equals seven divided by one. Engelmann then asks, "How can you turn seven into one?" and guides them, writing $7/7 = 1$. "Can you prove it?" he asks again. The class begins to chant in unison. "One over one equal one, two over two equal one, three over three equal one"—and having reached "seven over seven equal one," they are so full of revival spirit that they won't stop. Shouting louder and louder, having a rollicking time, they go on to "twenty over twenty."

Engelmann then draws a rectangle on the board, labels one side 4, another side b and the enclosed area 28. "How can I write that?" he asks. The children tell him, amid much noise: "4 × b [pronounced "buh"] = 28." "Then what is buh?" continues Engelmann. They count by fours: "Four times one equal four, four times two equal eight," watching the multiplication chart, until they reach seven. "You're tougher than a country cop!" exclaims Engelmann. After a few more exercises, the class is over. "Good job, gang!" says Engelmann, as the children recess for twenty minutes out-of-doors on monkey bars and swings.

Two hours of teaching like this require enormous endurance. It puts everyone—particularly the teachers—through the wringer. The noise assails one, the questions keep coming. There is so much activity that no one has time to be bored. "It's difficult to keep the class going at a pace so they learn more quickly than they forget," comments Mrs. Margaret Welsh, a teacher who has been with the project since its beginning. "There is so little time—everything you do has got to count. The singing, every activity, must be related to what you're trying to teach." She adds that for these children at home, to be good is to be quiet; here, "We make them speak out!"

"Our kids develop a tremendous morale," says Bereiter. "Something wonderful happens to their self-image. There is only one kind of challenge here—an intellectual challenge—and they come to welcome it." I commented on their boot-camp, Marine Corps zeal. "It's certainly not militaristic," demurred Bereiter, "but in contrast to other kinds of morale, this is an important one to have. Others are fairly effective too. Montessori, for example—a quiet, rather delicate atmosphere where each child is working quietly at his own things. But they don't learn how to talk there! It's essentially nonverbal. And verbal abilities are central ones: That's about the only thing that's been found out in thirty-five years' work of predicting success in school."

Does this morale, and the children's achievement, result from having male teachers around, I asked Engelmann? After all, many of them come from fatherless homes. "No—that's been highly overrated," Engelmann replied emphatically. "Just get teachers, male or female, who're not wishy-washy." In his opinion, the keys to the children's progress are the curriculum itself and the fact that they know what the rules are. Just as they learn without any rebellion that they can't go outside naked, these children learn things without strain because they know what they must do.

Some weeks earlier, in New York, a woman who works in the Board of Education's early-childhood department had told me, in tones of horror, that it was "absolutely terrible" to do what Bereiter was doing to three- and four-year-olds, and that if any body treated animals with equal cruelty "you'd call in the ASPCA!" She had not seen the program in action, she said, assuring me that she didn't want to see it, either. Though she was totally misinformed about it—for one thing, no three-year-olds are involved—her indignation was typical of many people in her field who find Bereiter's and Engelmann's ideas outrageous.

The two young men are certainly something of a phenomenon, having come at their subject from an entirely new angle. Instead of starting out with conventional learning theories, or some body of research, they asked themselves two questions: What do the children need to learn? How can it be taught to them in the time available?

The program is derived from sheer common sense, says Bereiter. If it is unique, it isn't because of the noise and the regimen, but because it is the only program that attempts to answer these two questions systematically—and then actually does what the answers imply. He thinks that anyone else who asked himself the same questions would come up with approximately the same answers if he pursued them far enough.

Originally, Bereiter was interested in literary creativity, Engelmann in philosophy. Bereiter took an M.A. in comparative literature, and after a stint in the Army spent two years teaching high-school English. He then went to the University of Wisconsin for a Ph.D. in educational psychology. Engelmann's interest in teaching was awakened by his work with his own two children—work which led to his controversial book *Give Your Child a Superior Mind*. He also made a film which demonstrated his techniques of teaching algebra. After Bereiter saw the film he persuaded Engelmann to join him at the Institute.

For a man trained in education, Bereiter was then reaching some strange conclusions. He had been trying out different methods of teaching reading to bright two- and three-year-olds. With one group he used a games method and with the other teaching machines. Despite the different methods, he recalls, both groups of toddlers ended up being *taught*, as if in a school, sitting at desks. This conflicted with everything he had read about young children, but it seemed to work best. It came as a shock to him.

"Having come through Education, I had lots to unlearn," he says wryly. "No—not child development, or I wouldn't have unlearned yet!" Fundamentally, the problem was to get over an embarrassed feeling about the act of teaching. Teaching implies, first, that the teacher is convinced the thing is worth doing, whether the child wants to or not, and, second, that the teacher knows *how* to teach—that his way, if not the best, is at least better than leaving things to happenstance.

In Bereiter's opinion, many attempts to allow a child freedom of choice stem from indoctrination in the idea that teachers are not qualified to make these choices. "Teaching is equated with 'playing God' in the eyes of lots of educators, and of most old-style child-development people," he says. "But I've finally come to an attitude that's more characteristic of other professional people, like physicians. I'd expect any competent doctor to make me well, whether I wanted to get well or not—and this is particularly true about children! I can quit smoking or not, but a child has got to take his medicine."

I blinked at the word "medicine," but Bereiter faced the issue squarely. "Here is the bind," he said. "Not all medicines have to be unpleasant. But if you feel that everything you do must be pleasant or interesting for the child, you've curtailed your freedom. Suppose you design a way to teach arithmetic that's on the whole very pleasant, what do you do when you hit a bad spot? That's where the method disintegrates. The simplest thing is to go ahead even if it is unpleasant, and get through it and on to something pleasant. Then the teacher has some freedom. Of course, we try to make the program pleasant for the kids, and to eliminate any dull or rough spots."

Engelmann spent his first summer at the Institute comparing the abilities of four disadvantaged Negro preschoolers and a few gifted children of Illinois faculty members. The differences astounded him. By the end of the summer he had worked out a remedial language program for the disadvantaged that laid the basis for much of the present project.

Following the lead of Robert Gagné, an Air Force psychologist who emphasized the need to define educational objectives through task analysis, Bereiter and Engelmann then began to study just what was lacking in the language of disadvantaged children. They found that such children can use language to get along socially, but when it comes to expressing ideas they are in trouble. Bereiter and Engelmann then decided to separate these two kinds of language, and teach only the second kind. They would not emphasize vocabulary, idioms, intonation, or accent, but language as an instrument of learning and thinking. They would not care much that a child did not know the word *sheep*—though most preschool teachers might react to such ignorance with shock—but they would make very sure that the child did understand such words as *not* and *or*, some of the most powerful logical tools in the language.

"If it is language as an instrument of social communication that separates man from apes, it is language as a tool of thought that separates civilized men from barbarians," declared Bereiter. "It is this latter use of language which, if I read my history correctly, was the legacy of ancient Greece."

In effect, they would teach English as a second language, emphasizing the kind of logical statement patterns used to teach foreign languages to college students. "When these children first came in, they couldn't utter or repeat a single statement," Bereiter points out. "They couldn't say, 'He's a big dog'; they said, 'He bih daw.' When asked to repeat 'It is in the box,' they'd become so confused by the number of words that all sounded the same to them that they'd be reduced to a stammer. They could not ask questions. The basics of foreign-language pattern drill have been around for a while, and our rationale is the same in one sense: The rules they must learn are learned by analogy. With young kids, you have no option —you can't *tell* them what the rules are. So you can either drill with things that all follow the same rule, as we do, or leave it to chance. Our goal is to speed up the learning."

The two Young Turks started their preschool project in November, 1964, and together they wrote a book, *Teaching Disadvantaged Children in the Preschool*, in which they answer some of their critics. They point out, for example, that a little stress is good for children so long as it is not due to fear of failure, concern over pleasing the teacher, or sheer competitiveness, but caused by curiosity or a desire to achieve competence. The idea is to make the children feel they are succeeding at something very tough—when, in fact, the problems are carefully geared to their capabilities.

Though their project does not have the "mother and her brood" atmosphere of many nursery schools, it does create very strong ties between the children and teachers because of their highly motivated, long-term involvement in a common task. Furthermore, the three-teacher arrangement seems to have important advantages for the children. They come to know each teacher well, but if a certain teacher does not relate well to the children, they can tolerate her and learn from her, but invest their emotional capital elsewhere. Thus potentially neurotic relationships can be avoided, and much less depends on the personal adequacy of each individual teacher. What these children really lack is not mothering, but almost always fathering, they add. Quoting Theodor Reik, the authors point out that motherly affection—generally indiscriminate and unearned—is essential to stability, while fatherly affection—discriminate and variable—is essential to growth.

What about creativity and self-expression? Engelmann and Bereiter do not believe that divergent thinking is fostered by simply allowing children to talk, paint, stack blocks, mold clay, and so forth. On the other hand, activities can be built into a teaching program that encourage the child to use what he has learned to create new things: inventing new verses for songs, generating explanations for events in stories, thinking up new words that rhyme or alliterate with other words.

Finally, what about the development of social skills and peer-group relations? The disadvantaged child, say Bereiter and Engelmann, needs to learn to relate to an adult as a pupil, and to other children as a fellow learner as well as a playmate. When a group has a clear-cut task to which all members are dedicated, maintenance functions are minimized and often seem to take care of themselves. Many traditional nursery-school classes, though they may provide an abundance of activities, have few tasks to mobilize the efforts of the children, and so the maintenance of social relationships becomes the major occupation. In such a situation the teacher is likely to develop a good deal of social skill, but it is doubtful whether the children will, because they are mainly manipulated by the teacher.

J. McV. Hunt, who is on the same campus and has visited the project often, says: "There is evidence of more change in Bereiter's school than in any other I've seen. When he set up his class last year, the children tested under age three on the Illinois Test of Psycholinguistic Abilities (ITPA). They didn't talk to each other at all except in single words and grunts. In each of two three-month periods of this school they gained about one year of psycholinguistic ability on the test."

The particularly rapid gains on one of the ITPA subtests—that dealing with "verbal encoding"—suggest that the training generalized beyond the simple language patterns in which the children had been coached, adds Dr. Hunt. This subtest requires the children to "tell me all about it" when they are shown an object, and scores them on the basis of how many different appropriate things they say. It is thus a fairly free, creative type of test. Bereiter concludes from these results that, paradoxically enough, the best way to teach young culturally deprived children to verbalize more freely and expressively—is to ignore the matter and concentrate on more fundamental language processes.

The single most impressive achievement of the children in his program, Bereiter believes, is that they now speak in sentences, and are thus able to "unpack" meaning from statements. By contrast, in most Head Start projects the children spend much time on puzzles, pasting, and other activities that do not require talking. "Frankly, Head Start doesn't look like an educational program at all," says Bereiter. "It's obvious to me that public medicine is the key issue there. Quite a bit could be done in eight weeks, though it's hard to convince people of this. If you start proposing intensive training in language or reading, they say, 'Now, all you're doing is starting first grade eight weeks earlier.' Yet even that could make a difference—after all, a child who entered first grade eight weeks after it had started would have a lot of trouble catching up. Also, Head Start has more teachers, and the child would get education of quite a bit higher quality."

Because their system worked so well with disadvantaged pre-schoolers, Bereiter and Engelmann decided to try it out with middle-class youngsters as well. They chose a group of four-year-olds as similar as possible to other middle-class children who were attending a local Montessori class, and had them start in October of 1965. The performances of the two middle-class groups were to be compared later.

How did the middle-class children take to it, I asked Bereiter. He smiled. They were a bit harder to break in, he admitted. They had some pretty well-established notion that this was a place to play. None of them had been to any other nursery school, but some had had Sunday-school experience. Because of their tendency to play, their greater spontaneity, and the fact that they were very verbal, it took one to two weeks to establish the routines. With the disadvantaged children, these were established right away.

Since he had overestimated what they really knew, he had to keep going backwards. He wasted a lot of time that way, and finally started at the same point as with the disadvantaged, but later, so that by the end of the first month the more advantaged children were far behind. Nevertheless, they overtook the others readily—they could go so much faster. Another difference was that with the middle-class children Bereiter tried out a phonetic alphabet called ITA.

As I soon found out, the more-privileged children create a different atmosphere in the classroom. In their arithmetic class a young male teacher was snapping his fingers in rhythm, leading a group of fresh faces as they counted by threes: 3-snap-6-snap-9-snap-12-snap . . . 27-snap-30-snap. "Now prepare to count down from twenty, while looking at the number board," he said.

"I don't need the number board to count from twenty!" one boy yelled—a comment that would have been unthinkable in the disadvantaged group.

"All right, then you look in the opposite direction," replied the teacher, concentrating his attention on the rest of the group.

"I want to count by fives now!" interrupted another boy.

In their language class, these children don't need to be taught to make statements. Although they are only four years old, their class resembles the kindergarten group's "causality." A teacher shows a book about dinosaurs and talks about their teeth. "Why do these dinosaurs have flat teeth?" she asks. Some of the children reply, "Because they are plant-eaters." "Dinosaurs are not living now," continues the teacher. "How do we know they lived?" Boy: "Because we find parts of them." The teacher then draws two small white squares, two large black squares, and one large white square on the board. Meanwhile, conversations start spontaneously among the children. Something in a drawing reminds a child of Superman. Others pick up the Superman theme. They want to talk of many things. It's all very social, like a party for them, and they resist the teacher's adherence to her curriculum.

"We'll talk about Superman later," says the teacher. "I'm waiting for squares right now. Let's speak about squares." The class takes awhile to settle down, but finally consents to pay attention. "Does *some* of them mean *all* of them?" begins the teacher. She draws a line around three of the squares and asks the children to define her selection: Did she include all the white squares, or only the small white squares? The children go along with her grudgingly. There is no urgency here—no rescue operation is required. One way or the other, one feels, these children will do pretty well in life.

As to the others—time is against the disadvantaged child, writes Bereiter. One becomes impatient with any teacher who wastes that precious time. The disadvantaged four-year-old, happily shoveling sand at a sand table, gives the impression that he will be four years old forever. But for the teacher to act as if this were true is disastrous. She should be constantly aware that the first grade is hurtling toward that child like an express train, and that the child's fate may well depend on what she as a teacher is able to do, and how quickly.

With this urgency in mind, I went to take another look at the poorer children's kindergarten in the spring, when only a few months were left before the end of the school year and their release from the program.

Over the months, the composition of the subgroups had changed: There were now eight pupils—more than half the class—in the top track, where previously there had been only four.

In the arithmetic class, the teacher is saying, "You can buy eight eggs for 56 cents. I want one egg. How are you going to figure it out?" She writes it out to help them: "$8e = 56$." "Count by eights," she reminds them. "How many times? Go!" Four of them push to the front, to be near the numbers chart. They count out loud and announce, "Seven!" "Good," says the teacher, and writes, "$e = 7$." But one little boy gets up and strides to the board. "You forgot to put this!" he says distinctly, writing in "¢" after the 7. "That's right!" agrees the teacher, looking pleased.

Engelmann then takes over the top group, scheduled to do causality, for its first lesson in definitions. He had explained his plan to me: The children must first put the thing in a class, then show how it differs from others of that class.

"What's a pistol?" he begins. The pupils answer things like "to shoot," or "bang-bang." "No," objects Engelmann, "first you tell me what class it's in." The songs have done their work, and someone replies at once, "Weapon." Engelmann then asks for the names of other weapons, getting "rifle" "sword," and "knife." He draws a big circle on the blackboard, divides it into four parts, and in each quarter draws a picture of one of the weapons suggested.

"Now," he says, "tell me about the pistol so I can cross these out, so I know it's different from these other weapons." Silence. "What does it shoot?" prompts Engelmann. "It *shoot!*" cries out a boy gleefully, thinking he has seen the light. At the same time, another boy, somewhat more sophisticated, shouts, "It shoot bullets!" "Right," says Engelmann, moving his finger as if he were pulling a trigger, "it shoots bullets." And he crosses out the sword and knife. "But now, wait a minute—what about the rifle?" he asks. "*Both* can shoot!" exclaims a boy. "So what's the difference between the two?" asks Engelmann. Long silence. They're really thinking—their concentration seems total. There is a feeling of suspense. To help them out, Engelmann says, "What if I had a pistol tha-at long?" and stretches his arms way out. "It wouldn't be true!" shouts a boy. Engelmann pretends to hold the long, long pistol with two hands. "Only one hand!" yells a kid. "Okay," says Engelmann triumphantly, "a pistol is a weapon that shoots and that you hold in one hand. This is the definition of a pistol." He asks a boy to repeat this definition—What is a pistol? Boy: "A pistol is a weapon what you shoot." Another boy adds instantly, "With one hand!"

"What is a rifle?" Engelmann asks next. "You hold it with two hands!" answers a boy. "A rifle is—" prompts Engelmann, pointing out that you hold some swords with two hands, too. (He demonstrates.) Finally he gets the correct definition out of them. It's a hard pull—as it would be with any group of five-year-olds. But it would have been totally impossible at the beginning of the year, and no first grade teacher in a slum neighborhood would dare attempt it.

During their reading class, the top-track children start out with flash cards printed in lower-case letters. "Lit, bit, sit, fit," they read. "That's good!" says the teacher. A boy hums to himself with satisfaction. The teacher then passes out books, and each child reads a line in turn: "Sit, Rags." "Sit on the mat." "Sit on it." "A pin is a bit of tin." They do it haltingly, but they are well on their way, and far ahead of many first-graders. "You did a good job today," says their teacher. The children rush out toward the cloakroom, with much yelping and scuffling.

Some need help in getting dressed, particularly one little boy whose coat is about four sizes too big for him, with sleeves so long that they hide his hands. As the children wait near the door of the room, the teacher brings them a box in which she had stored the prized possessions they had brought to school that day—a pitiful array of shapeless bits and pieces of wood or paper. Poverty is stamped on the clothes and gestures of the children who claim these playthings. They look more serious and a good deal tougher than middle-class youngsters of their age. But there is also an air of competence about them.

By the end of the year, this group of five-year-olds placed at mid-second-grade level in arithmetic and mid-first-grade level in reading and spelling on the Wide-Range Achievement test. The four-year-olds had gained an average of 17 points of IQ and scored at first-grade level in arithmetic, reading, and spelling. Both groups performed nearly on a par with gifted children of their age.

It has been said that anybody can do anything if he has only fifteen children and two teachers and $5,000 worth of materials. Bereiter's program requires no special equipment, but it does have three teachers for only fifteen children—an unusually high ratio—and it does require these teachers to be specially trained in the method. In this sense, it is far from cheap. Nor does anybody know yet how effective it will be in the long run. Will the children's confidence collapse when they are denied the support of this close-knit group, with its extra attention and many rewards? Will it survive twelve years in crowded slum schools that are geared to turning out failures? From another point of view, have they learned, deep down, to parrot unquestioningly whatever they are told by people in authority?

The answers will not be in for many, many years to come. It is not even clear yet whether the project itself—with its highly charged atmosphere, its mystique, its sense of excitement—can survive alone, or whether it depends on the presence of its two creators. Meanwhile, it looks as though some teachers will try to integrate some of these methods into their regular classrooms.

Recently, for example, the National Council of Teachers of English Task Force recommended that preschool curricula for disadvantaged children include some twenty minutes a day of the type of pattern drills pioneered by Bereiter and Engelmann —the kind of drills that teach children to master logic, not facts. It pointed out that attempts to engage children in conversation do not necessarily guarantee that they will pick up the needed language skills, any more than mathematics can be picked up through casual experience.

At the very least, then, the program is forcing responsible teachers of the disadvantaged to re-examine some of their cherished clichés. But most teachers remain violently opposed to it. They object for the sake of the children, whose individuality they believe would be threatened; and they object for their own sake, for similar reasons. This is not too surprising, since what Bereiter and Engelmann have done is to write a program very close in spirit to the bulk of those written for teaching machines and computers. It is equally rigid, logical, and efficient. The main difference is that instead of programming the "hardware," they have programmed the teachers. Naturally each teacher, being human, filters the program in a different way—but the similarity to machine programming persists, and it is bound to arouse some resistance.

Chapter 5

THE TALKING
TYPEWRITER

SHOULD early education push young children—or is there a low-pressure way to develop competence? Omar Khayyam Moore, the University of Pittsburgh professor who invented the talking typewriter on which children as young as three and four have learned to read, write, and compose poetry, firmly believes in the low-pressure way. He also wishes that people would pay less attention to the "hardware" and more to his responsive environments method.

This method consists of letting the child teach himself skills in his own way, without adult interference. In principle, at least, the child always takes the initiative. The environment—both man and machine—simply responds in certain ways, depending on what the child has done. This means that no two programs are alike—each child faces puzzles that are programmed just for him, and that keep changing as he goes along. He never needs to please an adult, or to achieve anything. But if he keeps at it, he gradually makes a series of interlocking discoveries about sounds, words, and sentences, much in the way that young children learn to talk.

Moore has found that children not only learn rapidly in this fashion, but also like it enough to keep coming back for more. Particularly between the ages of two and five, he believes, children are capable of extraordinary feats of inductive reasoning if left to themselves in a properly responsive environment. Unlike most adults, he says, children can and do enjoy learning.

Although he uses a machine, his approach thus seems much less mechanical than Bereiter and Engelmann's. They depend on praise and pressure from the teacher; Moore tries to eliminate all extrinsic rewards. They use predetermined sequences, making every child follow exactly the same path; Moore emphasizes that the coming revolution is individualized instruction— "and I don't mean just individual pace."

His own work, he feels, stems from the American progressive and pragmatic movements, as expressed by John Dewey and George Herbert Mead, and represents, for better or for worse, the lively part of the progressive tradition. "Now, for the first time in human history," he says, "you can have an educational scheme truly tailored to the individual person, even if persons occur by the millions. In the Dewey progressive scheme, the whole idea was just that; but it was merely a pious hope until technology made it possible."

On the technological side, Moore's system involves the talking typewriter—a loose term which may mean a slightly modified electric typewriter, plus dictation equipment, an exhibitor, and a human instructor (its original version), or a fancy, $35,000 automated machine called the E.R.E. (Edison Responsive Environment). Highly complex and subtle, the E.R.E. can be programmed to talk, play games, read aloud, take dictation, and show pictures. It boasts an electric typewriter with keys that cannot jam; a narrow window, through which letters, words, or sentences may be exhibited; a slide projector; a microphone; and a speaker—all connected to a small computer and weighing about 500 pounds.

Naturally, in a gadget-loving society, the E.R.E. has caught the spotlight of attention. But most of Moore's work was done with the earlier, inexpensive version of the talking typewriter, or with semiautomated models, in the use of which human teachers still played essential roles. He never tried to rely entirely on automated instruments. And since a separate program must be worked out for each child, the presence of a human being will continue to be necessary—at least with the younger children, and at least some of the time.

Yet people persist in seeing only a fabulously expensive machine which, they believe, does all the work of teaching by itself. And when educators see any machine that is supposed to help children learn something, they generally react either with contempt ("It's just another gimmick") or with fear that it will replace the teacher. Both these extremes ignore the fact that a machine—like a book—is only as exciting, rigid, provocative, or dogmatic as the ideas of the person who devises its program.

Like most inventors, Moore defies classification. A man of medium height and a quiet but intense manner, he comes from outside the world of teachers' colleges or even conventional psychology. Born in the small town of Helper, Utah (Omar Khayyám was his father's favorite poet), raised in Nebraska, he took his Ph.D. in sociology at Washington University in St. Louis, Missouri, and taught experimental sociology—a rare field—at Yale. Crossing into another discipline, he then became professor of psychology at Rutgers. Now, at the age of forty-six, he is professor of social psychology at the University of Pittsburgh, but on leave to do a large-scale study of his method for the Office of Economic Opportunity. Through it all, his main interest has been human higher-order problem solving—he turned to children only to investigate how they solve certain problems.

He began by studying how adults learn symbolic languages. He taught symbolic logic to Navy recruits by means of cubes with logical symbols, a record, a projector, and a program that ranks among the first examples of effective programming—the technique of presenting materials in sequences so precise that they can be used either within teaching machines or in self-teaching textbooks. But after a while he shifted his emphasis from deductive to inductive processes. His research with adults then became more and more difficult. What he needed was a lab in which an entirely new order of things had to be discovered—as if on the moon. Rather than create a whole new environment that was strange enough, Moore decided to go in for ignorant subjects. The most ignorant subjects, of course, were newborns. And the most practical time to start experimenting was when these children were walking and talking, at two or three.

This led to the Responsive Environments Project, a long-term research program which Moore began at Yale in 1959. One of the movies he made then, showing youngsters of two and three learning to read and write on an electric typewriter, caught the eye of a private-school headmaster, Edward I. McDowell, Jr., who invited him to set up a demonstration project at his school. Accordingly, with help from the Carnegie Corporation of New York, Moore opened a Responsive Environments Laboratory on the campus of the Hamden Hall Country Day School, a coeducational school for 340 children from nursery to twelfth grade.

The lab was a green prefabricated structure, with six soundproofed booths, which some sixty of the youngest children visited voluntarily every day. Its rules were simple: No child could stay longer than half an hour a day, though he could leave sooner if he wished. Since there was room for only six children at a time, they took turns coming, but were always free to pass up their turns.

On their first visit to the lab, the children were shown around by another child—part of Moore's plan to make them feel that the lab belonged to them. Parents were never permitted to see their own child in the lab. Even the regular teachers, whom the children might have wanted to impress or defy, were kept in the dark about their pupils' progress. A separate staff, made up largely of Yale graduate students' wives, was carefully instructed never to praise or blame any child. In Moore's words, "The lab represents thirty minutes away from the significant persons in the child's life—he is on his own, in a new environment, where all activity is carried on strictly for its own sake."

Sitting before a talking typewriter for the first time, the child was given no instructions at all. He soon discovered that this interesting, adult-looking machine was all his to play with. Whatever key he struck, the machine responded by typing the corresponding symbol in jumbo type, while a voice named the letter. Four days out of five, the voice was simply that of the human monitor sitting beside him, but if he was in the fully automated booth the machine spoke in the voice of whoever had programmed it. The typewriter's responses came as frequently as he desired. Especially for the youngest children, this sometimes proved irresistible: To test his new-found powers, one three-year-old gleefully struck the asterisk key seventy-five times in succession, while the poor human monitor repeated doggedly, "Asterisk, asterisk, asterisk, asterisk. . . ."

No two children proceeded in exactly the same way. Some tried each letter in a row, methodically; some played with numbers; others seemed to peck anywhere, at random. When their interest in this free exploration waned, the monitor switched a control dial and changed the game to a puzzle.

Without warning, a letter would appear on the exhibitor facing the child. The machine—or the monitor—would name the letter. And to the child's amazement, all the keys would be blocked, except the one that had been named. It was now a game of try-and-find-me. Eventually the child would hit the right key. Bingo! The key would go down, the machine would type the letter, which would be named again, and after a short interval another letter would appear on the exhibitor.

Urged on by curiosity and a desire to hit the jackpot, the children soon learned to find any letter, number, or punctuation mark that appeared and was named. Sometimes they tried to beat the machine—in fact, the voice could be slowed down or speeded up, according to the child, to make sure each one succeeded in naming some letters ahead of the machine. The children became familiar with various styles and sizes of type—upper-case, lower-case, cursive—as well as with handwritten letters, which could be flashed on the projector's screen. And they learned the sounds of the letters as well as their names.

At the same time, the children effortlessly learned to touch-type. One of the details they liked best about the lab was the chance to get their fingernails painted eight different colors, to match the colors on the typewriter keys. Each set of keys to be struck by a particular finger had its own color. Furthermore, the whole group of keys meant for the right hand responded to a slightly different pressure from that meant for the left. In this way they picked up the correct fingering technique without actually noticing it.

As soon as a child became expert at this game and the challenge diminished—this could be seen when his stroke count for the day decreased—the rules were changed once again. Instead of a single letter, a word would appear on the exhibitor. The word came from the child's own vocabulary, since one of the monitors had previously had him talk into a tape recorder for this very purpose. This ensured that the child was interested in this particular word, and also that he understood it.

Suppose a little girl had talked about her new baby brother. During her next session with the talking typewriter, after a little free-typing of letters and some try-and-find-me, she would suddenly see four letters on the exhibitor, with a red arrow pointing to the first one—B. The voice would say, "B-A-B-Y, baby." If she tried to type Y first, the key would refuse to go down. A would be blocked too. Only when she typed the letters in the right sequence would the keys respond, and then the voice would repeat "B-A-B-Y, baby," before going on to another word.

At no time was the child actually "taught" anything. For many children, this phase proved somewhat annoying; they would frequently ask, and get, a chance to go back to free-typing of letters. But after periods of varying lengths—days, weeks, or sometimes months—the child would suddenly realize that the letters he knew actually made up words that had a meaning, and that he himself could now write such words. This discovery is so elating that when it happens, children have been known to jump up and down in excitement, or run out of the booth to talk about it.

In Moore's opinion, this is the way to introduce learning to children—to make it so exciting that they are hooked for life. "It's an affront to your intelligence to be always told, always presented with everything," he says. Most systems in school alienate children for this reason. The children who are very able will learn anyway, but they won't like the learning part because it is too didactic.

Many details must be planned ahead to make the responsive environments system work. Every afternoon, the lab staff met to discuss the children's progress—an essential step, since the monitors took the children at random and had to know their idiosyncrasies, as well as the stage each had reached. Much depended on the sensitivity and intelligence of the lab supervisor. An experienced teacher, she decided when to shift the children from one phase to the next, on the basis of their performance and the monitors' reports.

The role of the monitor during lab sessions varied with the degree of automation in the booth. Sometimes she took over the voice part, speaking as gently and patiently as the E.R.E. Sometimes she operated the exhibitor by hand. When the child in her care used the fully automated booth, she watched through a one-way mirror, listening through a headphone, so she could come to his rescue if he needed help. A child was never simply left alone with the machine—he might need a handkerchief, or a change of program, or, depending on his mood, some human company. There was also the possibility, with the early models, of some mechanical malfunction which would have to be corrected immediately.

About once a week, each child at the lab played with chalk and a blackboard in the booth which had the least-automated equipment. Since the child had formed a mental image of various letters, sooner or later he would try to trace them on the blackboard's horizontal lines. At this point, the monitor would put the appropriate letter on the projector and suggest that he draw one like it. Thus, the child would learn to print as painlessly as he had learned to touch-type.

The dictation equipment in the talking typewriter was used nearly every day. Moore's plan was to give equal weight to all forms of language—reading, writing, speaking, and listening —so as not to produce speakers who have difficulty in writing, or tongue-tied writers. In many schools the curriculum for the first six grades tends to treat reading and writing as separate subjects, he says. Writing, in the sense of composing original stories, is yet another subject. Spelling and particularly punctuation are handled as special topics. The lab curriculum represents an attempt to deal with these skills and topics as part of an integrated complex. The child alternates between seeing words on the exhibitor, with the voice spelling them out, and hearing them on the tape recorder, as he himself had spoken them. He learns to write both kinds.

At first, the lab introduced the names of letters, so the children could know what to call them. Then it exposed them to the variety of sounds that went with these names. One of the many things a child induced, for example, was that "g" takes on different sound values in "gem" and in "game." He was provided with clean-cut cases, out of his own vocabulary. This led him to learn such letter combinations as "ea" in "ear" and "th" in "mother."

A further variation was to include words collected from stories that had proved interesting to children at the lab, so as to prepare them for actually reading these stories by themselves. Such word lists kept changing along with the children's interests, but nearly all of them included such necessities as "an, are, could, where, what, they." Occasionally some families of words were thrown in: "mat, pat, hat, rat." The words appeared in various forms: filmstrips, typed paper, handwritten cards.

Once over the hump of making and reading words, the children slid into whole sentences and paragraphs. Again they alternated between composing their own sentences and reading those taken from stories. Soon they became voracious consumers of written material. Seeing the rapid turnover of children at the lab—five every half hour, for about six hours a day—I asked how the lab kept up with all this. Where did most of the material come from?

"You get it from the kid," answered Moore firmly. "We've been telling people the same thing for years, but they just don't believe it! Of course, you must have some time with the child first, to listen to him. So one of our people will sit and listen to him, and record what he says on tape. Then his conversation will be broken down into its component words, sentences, and paragraphs."

Under the usual school system, Moore points out, a wave of children comes in in September, is treated impersonally, and many of them fall behind. By the fourth grade, when the failures become too obvious to ignore, the school begins its remedial steps. At that point, it takes its first close look at the child. The more deviant he is, the more attention he gets. The only way he can be treated as a person is to fail, says Moore, "and that's a strong motive to keep lousing up!"

It is one of the delights of this method that it shows clearly the infinite variety of things about which children care. A four-year-old boy who comes in with a bad cold eagerly confides his symptoms to the tape recorder and then flips a switch to hear himself played back: ". . . coughing and spitting the mucus." When the booth monitor writes some of the key phrases for him on a pad, he types them up with great self-absorption. Another child wants to compose endless shopping lists, mixing in bits of recipes. Another one free-associates: "mouse, letter, dog, octopus."

One spring morning, at Hamden Hall, I watched some of the youngest children, the nursery group, as they walked, skipped, or ran into the lab. First they went to a long table where a teacher painted their fingernails, dipping little brushes into open jars of bright-colored paints. Then they scattered to the six booths, to which they had been assigned at random.

An attractive little girl of four, who had been in the program nearly a year, sat next to a monitor and wrote her own sentences. She spelled the words out loud as she wrote: "After my nap I am going to the circus with my daddy. We s— I don't know how to spell 'saw'——[the monitor quietly said, "a," "w"] saw the parad ["Silent 'e,'" prompted the monitor] e yesterday. . . ." "Do you want to read it?" asked the monitor when the story was finished. The little girl shook her head. "I want to read a book!" she said. The monitor handed her *Time to Play*, a book labeled "Second Pre-primer." The child picked it up and began to read quite fluently, chuckling in a satisfied way as she turned the page, "Look here, here we come, look at Pepper and Sue."

Meanwhile, in the automated booth, another child typed away and the machine sounded out each letter that she struck. She wrote her brother's name, her own, several numbers and punctuation marks, then suddenly raised her hand. The monitor came in. "I want a book," the child demanded. "I want to read it by myself." She opened to a page and started reading into the mike: "We are all small. . . ."

Nearby, a boy was slowly making up some words on the typewriter, in capital letters. "You've got 'MON'; now let's finish it," said the monitor, pronouncing "th." The boy wrote "F." "No," said the monitor, "but you're close."

I glanced into the booth where children usually spent some time at the blackboard. Two little girls were taking turns reading into the mike. The words they read had been culled from one of their books: "Bat, bait, mat." They giggled and fooled around. "Okay, listen to yourselves," said the monitor, flipping some switches. The girls listened raptly. When it was over, they giggled again. Then they talked into the mike, telling each other stories about how their daddies mowed the lawn.

Obviously the nursery-group children were at many different levels. Some of them had started reading sentences early in the year, after only three or four months in the program, while others still struggled with simple words. These individual differences became ever more pronounced as time went on. In the next group, kindergarteners who had been there nearly two years, there were also some children who still worked with the easiest words.

In each case, the child's mood on a particular day had much to do with his performance. For example, a five-year-old boy from the kindergarten group came in morosely and typed, first his own name, then his sister's, then his brother's. Then he hesitated and did nothing for quite a long time. "Do you want to type your father's name?" suggested the monitor. "No!" shouted the boy, turning away from the typewriter altogether. The monitor then switched on the projector, with the beginning of a story that the boy could read. "I don't want to!" said the boy angrily. He glanced at a pile of books. The monitor picked up a few, suggesting *Curious George*. "I don't want to!" the boy said again, but less vehemently. He finally picked out another book by himself, and began to read *The Cat in the Hat Comes Back*.

Another kindergartener bounced in and asked for a book she had started the day before, C. N. Bonsall's *Who's a Pest?* She read with obvious enjoyment, stopping only to laugh at the story itself. Only a few words stumped her; at such times the monitor gave helpful hints. Then the child settled herself in front of the typewriter, picked out a word from the book—"extra"—and typed it. Next she selected another word—"and." Then, in a row, "dismay, yes, simple, even, noise, electric." There seemed to be some method to her selection, so after the session was over I asked the monitor about it. "Oh, it's a game," explained the monitor. "She likes to pick out words which start with the last letter of the word she has just finished typing."

Many of the kindergarteners read at first- or second-grade level, I was told. I watched one little girl as she read into a tape recorder from a standard second-grade filmstrip prepared by the Educational Development Laboratory of Huntington, Long Island. She read fluently: "Spot didn't like it because the ball would not roll where he wanted it to," then stopped abruptly and said, "I want to listen to it!" and had it played back.

The filmstrips were used for testing purposes. They showed that the first-graders read up to sixth-grade level, with the average around third-grade level, whereas the second-graders, who had been in the program two years, read up to ninth-grade level, with the average about sixth grade.

Far more impressive than these figures was the free use of language—spoken, written, typed, or dictated—by many children at the lab. The first-graders actually put out their own newspaper, *The Lab Record*, written and edited entirely by the children themselves. They dictated their stories into the tape recorder, typed them up, edited them, and typed the final copy. Those who could not yet read or write fluently enough stopped after the dictation phase. The newspaper contained drawings, riddles, and poems, as well as stories. One poem by a girl not quite six years old was entitled "A Duck," and read as follows:

> There was a duck,
> Who could kick.
> He had good luck,
> Because he was quick.
> He could run in a race,
> He would win.
> He would get some lace
> And a magic pin.

When I met the pint-sized poet she was engrossed in her daily session with the talking typewriter. A pretty little girl with long brown hair, she read fluently from the projector: "Once upon a time the African magician came to China to find a wonderful lamp . . ." and with dramatic flair continued, "Give me the lamp, and I will help you out." She then questioned the monitor about the story's plot, and answered the monitor's questions about the meaning of certain words. When she came out of the booth, she sat down with me in an empty office. I asked her if she wanted to be a poet when she grew up. "No," she replied without hesitation, "I want to be a housewife." Writing poetry was fun, she said, but the really nice part was being able to work on the newspaper "with Jeff," one of the editors. Did she prefer the lab when a monitor was in the booth with her, as today? She liked it best when she was alone in it, she replied emphatically, "so I can do *exactly* what I like."

Riddles were constant favorites: "Why does the firemen [sic] wear suspenders? *Answer:* To keep their pants up." "Why is grass like a mouse? *Answer:* Because the cat'll eat it."

Besides the newspaper, the children sometimes found special uses for their access to the lab. On one of my visits, a five-year-old boy whose mother was critically ill requested a specific typewriter, sat down before it and, in silent concentration, composed the following letter:

> Dear Mother,
> Get better soon!
> I love you very much and want you better very fast.
> I wanted to surprise you by typing you my first letter. Are you proud of me? I did it just for you Mother.
> I pray for you every night.
> Love and a big kiss from

After signing his name, he added: "I typed all of this letter by myself on the big grown up script typewriter."

Many reasons can be offered for these children's extraordinary facility with reading and writing: their high socioeconomic level (which may be necessary, but not sufficient); their innate ability (of the eleven children in the Lab's oldest group, two had IQ's in the genius range; however, the others were only slightly above the average for middle-class children); their freedom of action (similar to that of children in progressive nursery schools and kindergartens where they do not learn to read or write). But one factor cannot be ignored: the cumulative effect of exposure.

Because typing on an electric typewriter is so much easier for little fingers than making letters by hand, the children who came to the lab produced—and were exposed to—many more symbols than would be possible elsewhere. Even in ten minutes they could chalk up an impressively large stroke count. Those who stayed in the booth longer typed an average of 2,000 strokes a week, counting punctuation and spaces. They were surrounded by symbols, just as toddlers must be surrounded by words before they can learn to speak.

I visited the lab some three months after the beginning of the school year, and watched a boy of four and a half as he started banging on his talking typewriter energetically. He tried upper case and lower case; he ranged all over the keyboard; he typed the numbers from 16 to 20 in proper sequence; he played with the quotation marks; he wrote several nonsense words; then he typed carefully: "Barry is a RAT." The next few minutes were spent playing with the carriage return. He banged, and the machine's voice responded, "Carriage return" every time. Suddenly he added "and a cat." He was using correct fingering technique. During his twenty-seven minutes in the booth, he hardly stopped typing *something*. Later on, checking his records, Moore told me that the number of minutes the boy had stayed in the booth, and his stroke count, had gone up steadily since the beginning of the year. In his twelve weeks at the lab, he had struck a total of approximately 25,000 symbols—and by now he could read and write any simple sentence. Though he was bright, he did not test in the "gifted" range, which begins above an IQ of 140. He did have one incalculable advantage: permissive parents who laid great emphasis on intellectual skills, thus giving him much to relate to what he learned in the lab.

An even younger child, who did not attend the nursery school— the headmaster's little daughter, aged 2 years and 8 months—had taught herself on the typewriter all the letters in the alphabet, both upper- and lower-case, in about two months. She could also write some of them on the blackboard. I watched as she went into the automated booth and, with help because she was so small, hoisted herself on the chair facing the keyboard. First she pressed the carriage-return key a couple of times, then she banged on "c" and listened to the machine's voice. For awhile she hummed a tune. Next, she fiddled with a side lever. Finally she began to type a few letters rapidly, glancing up at the characters she produced and alert to the voice that came from the machine's speaker. After eighteen minutes in the booth, she raised her hand. A monitor came in to help her off the chair. "By-by," said the little girl, and walked out.

In general, those who start younger do better, says Moore. They have an easy, natural swing to their behavior. The older ones are more careful and deliberate. But a three-year-old will act as if he weren't paying attention. It's *really* free exploration, in a relaxed, fluid way.

At that age they can also tolerate a great many more errors than older children—or adults—will accept. Older, in this case, means children who have reached the ripe age of 6. One such newcomer to the lab was so afraid of making a mistake that he would hesitantly press a few keys and then run out to ask the monitor, "Am I doing it right?" He needed constant reassurance from an adult.

Moore's own daughter, Venn, started playing with the talking typewriter when she was 2 years and 7 months old. She could read first-grade stories before she was three. A very gifted child, she took part in Moore's first experiments with his method at Yale University, and starred in the short documentary movie that was made at that time. The movie shows her reading in a babyish voice, at two years, eleven months, typing sentences while singing out the names of the letters, and laughing or clapping her hands when she succeeds in finding the right symbol.

When I first met her, Venn was in Hamden Hall's first grade and acted as one of *The Lab Record's* editors. The other editor, Jeffrey, had also started using the talking typewriter during Moore's experiments at Yale. By then, both 6-year-olds could read seventh-grade books with pleasure. To test their skill, I opened a copy of *Scientific American* at random and asked them whether they could read it. They did so exuberantly, taking turns. Although they stumbled over some words which they did not understand, they could clearly handle anything phonetically.

Moore's respect for three-year-olds knows no bounds. "I wouldn't pit myself against a three-year-old any day, in meeting an utterly new problem or a radically new environment," he declares. "You've got your top problem-solvers there. By the time a child is three, he has achieved what is probably the most complex and difficult task of his lifetime—he has learned to speak. Nobody has instructed him in this skill; he has had to develop it unaided. In bilingual or multilingual communities, children pick up several languages, without accent, at a very early age. There's plenty of information-processing ability in a mind that can do that."

Unlike parrots, young children don't learn item by item, but by over-all search—they absorb whole patterns, Moore believes. Some of civilization's most important patterns are those which he calls "autotelic folk models." (Autotelic means that they contain their own goals and do not relate to immediate survival or welfare.) Through such models, children learn skills that will enable them to deal with the recurring problems of chance and strategy, with the puzzles posed by nature, and with various forms of art. Every society known to anthropologists has generated models of this sort. Simple forms of these models are internalized in childhood, says Moore, and more complex versions of them sustain us in adulthood. Without these abstractions, men would have been imprisoned in small groups, not unlike bands of especially intelligent baboons.

It is only recently that mathematicians have analyzed games of chance and of strategy, he points out. The mathematical theory of puzzles has not been very well worked out yet, and for esthetics there is no theory at all. But, so far, none of these four classes of models has required any technological expertise; for example, bits of wood will do for checker pieces. The models themselves are essentially static entities, in which the rules remain constant. They mirror the static quality of unchanging or imperceptibly changing societies, says Moore. In the past they have generally proved so successful that people had to be prohibited from playing too much. They have also served as a school for emotional expressions—the kind of school in which boredom is unlikely and uncontrolled emotional frenzy is forbidden. All in all, they have served man well—as did the Newtonian conceptions of space and time.

Today, Moore believes, dynamic models are needed. The rules of the game must keep changing, though not arbitrarily or irrelevantly. This will require extensive use of technology, since the players cannot be interrupted to explain each change.

From this standpoint, Moore comments that IQ tests measure only one aspect of people's abilities: the ability to solve short, static puzzles. They do not measure the ability to handle dynamic puzzles, or games of strategy, or esthetic objects. Better tests, like better models, would require a full use of modern technology.

Drawing on existing folk models, Moore tries to create as closely as he can the conditions of play: It has to be fun, and it must be fixed so there are no serious consequences. He also emphasizes inductive reasoning, "because in our world we can't stand pat. We have more new problems today than we can even name, and we must turn out larger and larger numbers of youngsters who can make fresh inductions about them, not just follow rules. This is our chief trouble today: technological change but intransigent behavior. It's too late for us—our generation can't make it. At best, we are just the transition group."

Creating the conditions of play is not so easy. As a hideous example of autotelic activities turned sour, Moore points to Little League play, which isn't play at all. Some parents can ruin almost any play situation, he says.

Children often seem to forget something they knew well before; at such times, it is particularly difficult for adult human beings to refrain from "helping" them. One of Moore's recent movies shows a little girl who suddenly forgot how to switch the keyboard to lower case. Until then, she had operated all the keys with ease, but now, after writing an upper-case "T", she did not know what to do. "Lower case," said the E.R.E. machine. The little girl explored the keyboard at random, but to no avail—all the keys seemed locked. About every fifteen seconds, the machine quietly repeated "Lower case," as a reminder. To an adult observer, the situation was almost intolerable. One wanted to run into the booth and show the child what to do. But the little girl did not seem at all concerned. After a moment's hesitation, she calmly began to try out all the keys systematically, column by column, until at last she hit the right one. At once, the machine responded, the pointer moved to the next letter on the exhibitor, and the voice simply sounded it, "o," as if nothing had happened.

In the privacy of a booth, children who don't understand very quickly need not be embarrassed or suffer from constant comparisons with the fast learners. The talking typewriter has infinite patience. It plays no favorites. It never tires of repeating things.

It never gets angry, and no child need feel anxious about losing its love. Thus, the slower children are not deprived of the chance to make their own discoveries, and the brighter ones can proceed without boredom.

So far, only a handful of mentally retarded children have tried out Moore's method. The results have been encouraging. A boy with an IQ of 65, for example, took nine months to learn what the brightest children had learned in three weeks—but eventually he got there, without any pressure, and learned to copy simple words, sentences, and stories. Moore's method thus holds hope for many kinds of retarded or handicapped youngsters—not just normal preschoolers. It can also be used to present foreign languages to students of all ages.

As a lesson in patience, all the monitors in the Hamden Hall Lab spent some time observing the fully automated E.R.E., so as to model their behavior on it. Nevertheless, there are certain limitations to human beings in this situation. Especially at the beginning, when a child is actively exploring the keyboard, a human instructor has a hard time keeping up with him. The faster a child goes, the more difficult for the monitor to keep up—or to remain calm and impersonal about it. Sometimes the child spends weeks testing the monitor's patience in this way.

It was to get around this problem that Moore and Richard Kobler, an engineer who is now manager of the Thomas A. Edison Laboratory of West Orange, New Jersey (a part of the McGraw-Edison Company), together invented the E.R.E. machine. The first prototype became available in 1961.

As Kobler puts it, the child who faces an E.R.E. is "in a monastic condition, in which nothing counts but the interplay between him and the machine. . . . He can *attempt* many errors during the phase with blocked keys, but he is not allowed to *execute* these errors. And so it becomes something very private: Nobody knows whether he made a mistake. He can only execute successes—but maybe after intensive inner battles, of the kind that belong to man's greatest experiences."

However, the E.R.E. could be programmed in countless different ways—even with electric shock or with pellets, Moore points out. It can be made rude, impatient, insulting, or even cruel. People who buy the machine sometimes do not realize they are merely buying a blank page—Moore's program does not come with it. The machine is easy to program from the technical point of view: The teacher or monitor simply puts one of the blank program cards into the typewriter, sets a few dials, and types out what he wishes, up to 120 words per card; these will then appear in any desired sequence on the exhibitor, and will also control the operation of the typewriter keys. The audio part is encoded by speaking into a microphone. The real problem is deciding what to program. To many teachers, the temptation is nearly irresistible to use the machine merely to present traditional, formal instruction in a more efficient form. Because of the time and labor consumed in programming, they would dearly like to have a program that could be applied indiscriminately to all children.

This is precisely where Moore's method differs from other forms of programmed instruction or teaching machines. It differs so much, in fact, that according to P. Kenneth Komoski, who evaluated such methods as president of the nonprofit Center for Programed Instruction at Columbia University's Teachers College, Moore does not have a "teaching" machine at all; he has a "learning" machine. While teaching machines generally make students come up with the right answer by leading them in a straight line from one little piece of information to the next, Moore's system gives children the opportunity to preserve a natural, inquisitive attitude.

Moore himself says that the other types of programming are too didactic. They inculcate a method of search that is prejudicial to finding a creative solution. The programmer takes a godlike position with relation to his subjects: He plans in advance, not the general environment, but the detailed steps they must take. This makes no provision for the students' possible contribution—for the possibility that they may come up with a solution he hasn't thought of. "It also presupposes," says Moore, "that we have some theory about human learning that is adequate—well, we don't."

He compares his system to a matrix, or a spider web. The others, he says, do not allow browsing; they are really a return to the scroll, over which books were an improvement. Why have an electronic scroll? asks Moore.

Moore's goal, then, is to produce independent thinkers—not to stuff any child with rules or facts. This has been widely misunderstood. Frequently it is the disciplinarians, those who want skills taught in a hard, didactic way, who are most attracted to the idea of using a machine. The progressives, who should favor whatever increases the child's individuality, tend to like programs that postpone intellectual actvity. "Everyone's on the wrong side," complains Moore. "This is really an ultraprogressive program. It's too bad people can't rationalize their positions better."

Since the lab took up no more than half an hour a day, the children still had their sandbox, paints, and other time-honored preschool activities. In fact, the lab actually allowed the prolonging of some of these things. As traditionally handled now in the nursery schools, at least the children are free, though they receive little intellectual stimulation. But in the first grade the game is over. At the very time when the child is becoming interested in the wider world around him, he must divorce himself from such matters and confine himself to squiggles. He must learn the alphabet, learn to print, and because of his low skill, read baby stories that are not appropriate for him. All of this takes so long that many important things are dropped as frills—painting and music, for instance. No wonder so many children develop a hatred for intellectual work early in school, says Moore.

By contrast, the first-graders who went to the lab had plenty of time for what is normally called enrichment, since their teacher did not have to drill them in reading and writing. The children read fourth-grade geography books, listened to music and poetry, played games, and went on field trips. Each one also read up on specific subjects that interested him particularly— boats, rockets, the moon.

"People used to ask me, What in the world will they do in first grade?" recalls Moore. "A year later, they asked, What in the world will they do in second grade?"

The second grade that evolved for the lead group from the lab was, in fact, so unusual that it nearly split Hamden Hall into two warring factions. Since the regular second-grade curriculum was obviously unsuited to them, a special class for only nine children had to be conducted in a separate building, with a separate teacher who had formerly been a booth monitor.

When I first visited this class, the children were listening to a record of Robert Frost reading his own poetry—"Stopping by Woods on a Snowy Evening." "It will take a little time to get used to his voice," said the young teacher, "so I'll read it, and then we'll listen again." Meanwhile, she passed around the record cover, with a picture of Frost. After the second hearing, she began to ask questions. "Miles to go before I sleep—what would you say this means?" she asked the class. Some children suggested "before night" and "before he falls asleep." One girl gasped, "Oh, I know! Before he dies." "Right," said the teacher, "and what do you call that?" A bucktoothed little blonde with a high-pitched voice piped up. "It's a euphemism!" she said. The children were all seven years old, except one girl who had just turned eight. They launched into a lively discussion of "why he said that when he's so old," as one boy put it. After a few more questions, the teacher asked, "Now, do you want to hear it again?" "Yes!" shouted the class. And in utter silence they listened: "The woods are lovely, dark and deep. But I have promises to keep,/ And miles to go before I sleep,/ And miles to go before I sleep."

In general, she tried to steer away from themes of death or growing old, the teacher later explained. But she did pick interpretive, rather than just descriptive, poetry, and by now the children understood the meaning of such terms as onomatopoeia and alliteration. She had read them some Tennyson, Shelley, Byron, and Wordsworth; many questions had been asked back and forth. It was Moore's idea to read them adult poetry, not just childish, sing-song verses.

"Ancient Chinese proverbs are particularly useful," added the teacher, Mrs. Anne Schrader. "They're excellent to make the children find their own interpretations. Then they invent their own proverbs." At times the children solved crossword puzzles which she made up for them, using words they had just come across.

Their day started with their least-liked subjects: penmanship and arithmetic. To make this more pleasant, Mrs. Schrader always played music for them while they worked—"Carmen," "Victory at Sea," "The Sorcerer's Apprentice," and other favorites. Each child worked on his own, generally with third- or fourth-grade workbooks. After that came vocabulary or poetry, and then recess.

I went down to the basement, drawn by the noise of children at play. "Here we go Loopy Loo! Here we go Loopy La!" sang the kids at the top of their lungs, trying to outdo the record player and swinging each other about.

Exhausted, yet refreshed, the children trooped back to their classroom, still full of fun. After some shuffling of chairs, they formed into three small groups; in each group a child began to read aloud—not *too* loud, so as not to disturb the other groups—from a book. A boy started reading from *The Brave and the Free*, a book of stories designed for sixth-grade reading programs. He read very fluently to the last paragraph on the page, as three little girls listened. When he stopped, the little girl to his left picked up the book and continued much more slowly, in a high-pitched voice. "All right, go ahead!" impatiently muttered another girl, who was interested in the story. The child tried to read faster, but stumbled over some words, so the first boy complained that he couldn't catch what she was saying. She finally settled down to a comfortable pace, and read to the end of the page. The other children took their turns. Occasionally they corrected each other's pronunciation ("Not pro-fit'-able, pro'-fit-able!"), but without animosity. At the end of the story the children took turns asking each other questions about what they had read. "What does 'Zowie' mean?" asked the boy. "It's something you say when you don't know what to say," replied the high-pitched girl. The boy was not satisfied. "There are many other words you could say instead," he argued. They went and looked it up in the big Unabridged Webster's which lay on its stand in the front of the room, next to a relief globe of the world.

After lunch, the children had music or art with the regular teachers, then gym, French, and their daily session at the lab. They no longer needed the automated typewriter—in fact, this would slow down their typing, since the keys were set to give the voice enough time to respond. But they did read books on subjects they found particularly interesting; they did use the recording and dictation equipment, and they worked on their newspaper. (By then, the new first grade had a newspaper of its own.) One child wrote: "Haiku is Japanese poetry. The form of it is, the first line has to have five syllables, the second line has seven syllables, the last or third line has five syllables like the first line. It has to have three lines, but it isn't supposed to rhyme." And then she composed her own haiku:

> Ivy on a wall
> Like wee little animals
> Climbing to their homes.

The regular teachers at Hamden Hall, meanwhile, watched these goings-on with dismay—and often a good deal of hostility. To them, the lab was an intrusion: Some of them had been at the school as long as twenty-seven years. They complained that the children who went to the lab were hard to handle as a group. "They all want individual attention because they're used to this one-to-one relationship," said one teacher. "They can't wait— they all want *their* table to be the first to get books."

"It's all too permissive," grumbled another teacher. "The children are less mature. When I was in public school, you had to finish one level first before going on to the next. Here they read one page of a second-grade workbook, and they say it's too easy, they want to go on to a higher level! They never finish anything—they just claim they've *done* that level!"

One teacher who taught the traditional first grade said, "They're reading at third-grade level in my class too, without the lab!" A science teacher commented that the lab group couldn't add or subtract properly; all they knew was how to work with Cuisenaire rods.

"I had to slap Jimmy once because he wanted to push all the buttons in the French-language lab," recalled the French teacher.

The school was soon so split on the issue of the lab that it became a political act for a teacher merely to visit the place— and during the three years of the demonstration program very few teachers did visit. Then the money ran out. The board of trustees decided it could not afford to continue the program, which cost between $25,000 and $30,000 a year (about $500 per child), all by itself. The parents of children in the top elementary and high-school grades were totally uninterested in the lab. The parents whose children did attend the lab volunteered to raise most of the money for the program, but the trustees rejected their offer. "There were no long-range plans for interweaving these children with the school," the board's president, G. Harold Welch, Jr., told me later. "There comes a point—about the third grade—when we wouldn't have enough students for two different third grades, because of the high mobility of parents. We have to have a single track."

Meanwhile, the school's headmaster, who had been closely associated with the lab, was forced out. McDowell had invited Moore in the first place and had two of his own daughters in the program. He described the lab as a gentle, humane environment in which young minds and emotions could and did flower. He believed that the kind of individualized instruction provided by the lab would lead to an ungraded school system all the way up the line. Educationally this is nothing new, but administratively it's quite a problem. Together with Moore, he formed an independent foundation, the Responsive Environments Foundation, Inc., in Hamden, Connecticut, to continue the work with different groups of children. And although the two men later parted company, McDowell remains convinced that the responsive environments method is "the soundest thing I've heard of in education. I've seen nothing since that comes close to it."

Toward the end of Moore's three-year demonstration at Hamden Hall, he asked the Educational Testing Service of Princeton, New Jersey, to come and test the lab children, because he wanted some outside confirmation of how well they were doing. Dr. Scarvia Anderson, E.T.S.'s director of curriculum studies, selected two standard achievement tests that are normally given to children in the fourth, fifth, and sixth grades. She then administered these tests to the second-graders who had attended the lab. One test—the Sequential Test of Educational Progress (STEP)—required the children to read a paragraph, read some questions referring to it, and select the correct answers to these questions. Six of the eight children she tested with it scored in the 80th to 99th percentile, far above the median for a national sample of fourth-graders, and two of them were above the median for eighth-graders. In another form of the STEP, the listening form, the examiner read both the text and the questions; the children were required to select one of four written answers. The entire class scored well above the median for fourth-graders on this test, and half the class scored above the median for eighth-graders.

From another point of view, Dr. Edith Lisansky, a clinical psychologist who tested the children at regular intervals, found that their Rorschach tests tended to show greater richness and better balance as they advanced in the program.

Moore collected much data on the children in the lab, but since it was a pilot project rather than an experiment comparing two groups of youngsters, he used this information only to change his procedures and equipment as he went along. He never published any detailed description of his method or its results. Though hundreds of educators visited the Hamden Hall lab, there are no written guides for teachers who may wish to duplicate what he did there.

This has produced enormous confusion among teachers, administrators, and prospective buyers of the E.R.E., who are led to believe that the machine alone can perform miracles. Educators who want to watch Moore's techniques in action can go to his foundation in Hamden, where a reduced staff works with some twenty to thirty children a day, using both automated and non-automated equipment. But most people find it easier to attend one of the demonstrations and sales talks offered by the distributors of the E.R.E. in New York City.

The greatest source of confusion has been the matter of automation. Moore's position is that nobody has yet found the optimal mix of automated and nonautomated equipment. This may actually vary with each child. At Hamden Hall he had at most a ratio of 1 to 4—and much of the time the machine, a prototype, was not working at all. At his foundation, the ratio is now 1 to 2—one automated booth for two that are nonautomated. Under his present plans the fully automated equipment will not be used more than half the time.

The E.R.E. was designed as a research instrument, Moore adds. Its cost makes it prohibitive as standard equipment in schools. Together with the engineer, Richard Kobler, he has been working on much cheaper devices that will perform some of the E.R.E.'s functions. One of these, about to be released, consists of a special surface on which a child could trace letters or write words with a stylus, and get a spoken response. Moore visualizes it as a classroom aid in a variety of kindergartens.

As to the responsive environments method itself, the question remains whether it is well suited to mass use. An experiment now in progress in Chicago should furnish some answers. In a desperately poor neighborhood called the Marillac area, 120 youngsters of three and a half and four have started using both automated and nonautomated talking typewriters under a program sponsored by the Cook County Department of Public Aid, with funds from the OEO. Their parents are either functionally or totally illiterate. The children's progress will be compared with that of a matched control group. During the late afternoon and evening, the Chicago Board of Education uses the same equipment to teach reading to school dropouts and illiterate adults. Each person's program is tailored individually. Moore is chief adviser for this experiment, which is expected to provide detailed statistics from various kinds of tests.

Moore's work thus represents a gallant effort to tame the products of modern technology, and make them serve the interests of each individual child. Throughout the country, big business is preparing to enter the field of education with computers and automated equipment. Most of these plans call for fitting strict programs onto whatever machine the company wants to sell—thus locking the student into a rigid system that demands total conformity. Going against this powerful tide, Moore remains concerned above all with the uniqueness of the learner.

Chapter 6

THE AMERICANIZATION

OF MONTESSORI

NEITHER Bereiter nor Moore has yet had much impact on pre-school education. The influence of the Montessori revival has been phenomenal, however, despite violent disagreement on whether the method was fifty years behind the times way back in 1915, or whether it was at least fifty years ahead. Some three hundred Montessori schools have sprung up in the United States in the past few years, surpassing by far the number established during the first wave of American enthusiasm for Montessori in the early part of the century.

"Tell us all about it. Is it really wonderful? Or is it just a fad?" the writer Dorothy Canfield Fisher was asked by her friends in 1912, when she returned from a long visit with Dr. Maria Montessori in Rome. The questions have scarcely changed since then. But few teachers still have open minds on the subject, having learned too well that Montessori was "disproved" years ago by educational philosophers such as William Heard Kilpatrick, who stressed children's social development. Very few teachers of preschool children have actually observed Montessori classes in action. Their training in teachers' colleges, however, leads many of them to reject her method outright, in a sort of neurotic overreaction.

As a result, parents of middle-class children have taken the lead in the Montessori revival. In many cases, the new schools were actually started by parents' groups for their own children. Of all the thousands of Head Start centers around the country, only a handful have been run on Montessori principles, and few of the burgeoning classes for disadvantaged children have used her methods.

Yet Montessori's greatest achievement was her success with children from the slums. This is, in fact, her major relevance today.

She showed how to run model day-care centers for children from three to seven, in districts where no one dared go about unarmed at night, and how to deal with what she called, in 1908, "a new fact which was unknown to past centuries, namely, the isolation of the masses of the poor"—none other than what modern sociologists have rediscovered as alienation.

Dr. Montessori educated these children so well, in an ungraded classroom, that she foresaw that the entire elementary school would have to be changed as a result. The first grade would disappear, since her school would take care of all it taught, and "the elementary classes in the future would begin with children such as ours who know how to read and write . . . who are familiar with the rules of good conduct and courtesy, and who are thoroughly disciplined in the highest sense of the term, having developed, and become masters of themselves, through liberty." Among these children's other virtues, as she described them, they "pronounce clearly, write in a firm hand, are full of grace in their movements . . . and possess the power of spontaneous reasoning."

The chief attraction of Montessori for middle-class parents is the fact that many children in Montessori classes do learn to read, write, and count at a very early age. Nevertheless, this is far from the goal of a Montessori education. Montessori's own aims, as expressed through her books, were much loftier: She wanted her charges to become as powerful in their concentration, as independent of spirit, as strong of will and as clear of thought as the world's greatest geniuses. She noted that many major discoveries stemmed from such virtues as independence and persistence. Newton discovered gravitation by thinking about why an apple fell on him from the apple tree. "The environment sometimes rewards 'small reasonings' of this kind in a surprising manner," said Montessori. "Simplicity is the guide to discovery; simplicity which, like truth, should be naked."

She saw the child of three as carrying within him "a heavy chaos." "He is like a man who has accumulated an immense quantity of books, piled up without any order, and who asks himself, 'What shall I do with them?'" Culture, she said, is not the accumulation of knowledge, but "the prepared order" in the mind which is to receive such knowledge. Her goal, then, was to train children to be like connoisseurs: so sensitive to the specific attributes of things around them, and so expert in classifying them, that everything would possess interest and value for them.

They would learn all this freely—but in a specially "prepared environment." She coined the motto "Things are the best teachers." And she invented the richest array of educational toys seen to this day—hundreds of simple puzzles and games designed to guide the child's progress and make him truly independent, both physically and mentally: buttoning frames; lacing frames; series of pegs with corresponding pieces to develop the concept of numbers; weights to be fitted into progressively deeper or wider holes; map puzzles with small knobs, to develop the kind of dexterity required for writing, while incidentally learning geog-raphy; the famous sandpaper letters which a child could trace with his fingers until the movements of forming each letter became permanently engraved in his memory. After playing with these sandpaper letters for a few months, children would often begin writing so naturally that they believed it had come to them just because they had reached the right age. Montessori's fertile mind produced a steady stream of new materials, each serving several purposes at once, each leading from the sensory to the symbolic, each preparing the child for a higher level of understanding.

Her equipment always allowed the child to work at his own pace, though it urged him to perfect himself. The materials were largely self-correcting, requiring a minimum of help from the teacher—usually just a demonstration, at the beginning, of how the materials were to be used. Thus each child could choose from such variety that forty children in the same class might well be occupied with forty different tasks.

Since the children did their own learning, Montessori invented a new role for the teacher. The teacher would no longer dominate the stage with her "patronizing, enfeebling protection." She would not be a substitute mother, or the sole dispenser of knowl-edge. Instead, she would be a directress, guiding the independent work of her charges, and her chief qualification would be a keen power of observation.

When, in 1912, Dorothy Canfield Fisher visited a Montessori classroom for the first time, this was what struck her most: "There seemed no one there to push the children or to refrain from doing it. That collection of little tots, most of them too busy over their mysterious occupations even to talk, seemed, as far as a casual glance over the room went, entirely without supervision. . . . In our town, where we all know and like the teachers personally, their exhausted condition of almost utter nervous collapse by the end of the teaching year is a painful element in our community life. But I felt no impulse to sympathize with this woman with untroubled eyes who, perceiving us for the first time, came over to shake hands." She also noted that the teacher seemed free of that "lion-tamer's instinct" to keep a hypnotic eye on the "little animals," so marked in the other instructors the author knew; she simply turned away from the children while she spoke, and none of the children appeared to notice that the teacher's back was turned.

In those days it was common school practice for small children to be kept silent and motionless at their desks for hours on end, listening to the teacher. Rows of pupils were confined in this posture for such long periods that physicians began to complain about the extensive curvature of the spine that the schools were producing, and special rehabilitation classes were needed to correct the spinal deformations caused by the desks.

Montessori suggested that children be given instead the right to move about freely, to lie on the floor on little mats if they wished, or to use movable, child-sized tables and chairs. She fought for their right to a free choice of tasks. She fought for their right to make a moderate amount of noise. At a time when discipline and "breaking the child's will" loomed as major issues, she devised ways of developing each child's strength of will—and the children in her classes responded with marvelous self-control.

Children are really patient and gentle creatures, Montessori declared. They have been much maligned. Their overriding aim in life is simply their own self-development—their "autoeducation." In this, Montessori paralleled the progressive educators who later became her bitterest enemies. Yet she differed on several essential points, particularly in her determination not to leave this autoeducation entirely to chance. If the children were to have freedom, she argued, then the environment had to be very carefully planned for them. She spoke of the soaring death rates among small children in the days before rational public-health measures were adopted. Similarly, she said, rational measures were needed to prepare the environment for good mental growth.

Spoken like a pediatrician: Maria Montessori (1870–1952) was, in fact, Italy's first woman physician. In her youth she had defied violent criticism to enter the University of Rome Medical School, earning the first M.D. degree it had ever awarded to a woman. She continued to display this independence throughout her life. While visiting mental hospitals as an assistant doctor at the University Psychiatric Clinic, her first job, she became interested in the large number of retarded children who were mixed in with the insane for want of any better place to put them. Though her fellow doctors spoke of these children's deficiencies as medical problems, she concluded that the problems were not medical, but pedagogical. Thereupon she decided to study education. She rediscovered the methods of Dr. Édouard Seguin (1812–1880), the great French physician who had developed a complete educational system for retarded children a half-century earlier, but whose work had been largely forgotten or misinterpreted. She also studied the work of Jean Itard, an even earlier French pioneer, from which she learned that clinical observation was just as important in education as in the treatment of the sick. She began to lecture Roman teachers on methods of observing and educating the retarded.

At the age of twenty-eight, she became the director of a new State Orthophrenic School which took over the education of all the children whom the elementary schools considered hopeless, as well as the retarded children who had been scattered in the insane asylums of Rome. Day and night, for two years, she worked with these children and trained their teachers. Guided by the work of Seguin and Itard, she created a great variety of educational materials of her own. She also tried an original method of teaching the retarded to read and write. Finally the retarded children whom she had taught took public examinations for primary certificates and, in a series of resounding victories for her method, passed the tests as well as normal children.

To the public, this seemed a miracle. But for Montessori it was a cause for worry. "While everyone was admiring the progress of my idiots," she wrote, "I was searching for the reasons which could keep the happy, healthy children of the common schools on so low a plane that they could be equalled in tests of intelligence by my unfortunate pupils!"

Trusting in her own logic, Montessori then decided to devote herself to normal children. The next seven years were spent in study, as she took courses in experimental psychology at the University and conducted her own research in the elementary schools.

At this point her path crossed that of a Roman entrepreneur who was looking for ways to restrain the little vandals in his new housing projects. With their parents out at work all day, hordes of preschool children spent much of their time defacing the walls there, fouling the stairways, and doing other kinds of costly damage. Better spend the money to prevent the damage, he concluded. He therefore asked Montessori to take over the management of what he visualized as a large room in each housing project, where the children could be kept out of mischief until their mothers returned from work.

From Montessori's point of view, this was an ideal experimental group. When her first *Casa dei Bambini*, or Children's House, in such a project opened in 1907, she found waiting for her "sixty tearful, frightened children, so shy that it was impossible to get them to speak, with bewildered eyes, as though they had never seen anything in their lives." They had some traits in common with the mentally retarded, she realized—their short attention spans, for example, and their language defects—but she soon became even more impressed by the differences between them: When she had used her didactic materials with the retarded, the puzzles and exercises merely made education possible; but when she used this equipment with normal children, she found it stimulated them to teach themselves. "This fact is one of the most interesting I have met with in all my experience," she declared. It convinced her of the need to give normal children as much freedom as possible.

The slum children were much younger than the retarded youngsters she had worked with before. At the beginning, therefore, Montessori had no intention of teaching them to read or write. "Like everybody else," she said, "I held the prejudice that it was necessary to begin as late as possible the teaching of reading and writing, and certainly to avoid it before the age of six." But soon the children, as well as their parents, were begging her to teach these skills.

After a fruitless search for someone who would manufacture a large and elaborate alphabet for them, similar to the one she had used with retarded children, Montessori decided to cut her own letters out of paper and sandpaper, with the help of her teachers. This was how she stumbled on her famous movable alphabet and sandpaper letters. The former could be multiplied as frequently as desired and used by many children at once, not just to recognize letters, but to compose words. The latter provided an effective guide for the little fingers that touched them. Only after she had tried these out did Montessori realize that, far from having devised a makeshift arrangement, she had invented a powerful new tool for learning.

The letters were all lower case. As the method evolved, the directress would take two of the sandpaper letters at a time—starting with the vowels—and present them to a child, teaching only their sounds, not their names. She would also show him in what direction to trace the letters with his fingers. In this way the child learned three things at once: what the letters looked like, how they sounded, and how they felt. This last impression, muscular memory, said Montessori, often superseded that of either sight or sound in small children.

In presenting the consonants, the directress would add a vowel sound and pronounce the syllable as a whole. But no particular rule was followed as to the order in which the letters should be presented, since Montessori wished to let the child's curiosity be his guide.

The next step was to ask the child to find the letters that the directress pronounced: "Give me o! Give me i!" If he failed, he was not told he was wrong, but the lesson was ended for the day. A cardinal rule was never to insist on teaching when the child did not respond readily.

Finally, the child was asked to sound out the letters to which the directress pointed—"What is this?" As soon as he had learned one consonant, he could begin to compose his own words.

By the time a child could recognize letters by touch alone, even when blindfolded; compose words easily with the movable alphabet; and fill a geometric inset with neatly parallel lines, he was ready for what Montessori called the "explosion into writing." One day he could not write by himself—and the next day he could: It was as simple as that.

Montessori reported countless episodes of the excited joy of a child who wrote a word for the first time; she compared such children to hens who had just laid an egg. Sometimes, she said, no one in the school could escape the noisy manifestations of the little one, who would force everybody to come and admire his work, tugging at their clothes if they resisted. For a while after learning this first word, the child would write everywhere—on the blackboard, on the window shutters, on the doors. Mothers complained that their children wrote even on the crusts of their bread loaves. Later on, Montessori learned to control this phenomenon by encouraging the children to start writing *before* they had the entire alphabet at their disposal.

Nothing else in the Montessori system seems to have made as much impression on the public of her time as this progress in reading and writing. Largely because of the children's feats in this line, the Casa dei Bambini was soon swamped with visitors from all parts of the world, and hundreds of books and articles were written about it. Montessori's work was described, once again, as miraculous.

At the invitation of publisher S. S. McClure, she visited the United States in 1913. Later, she was entertained at the White House, and lectured to overflow crowds at New York's Carnegie Hall. From 1913 to 1915, the high point of American enthusiasm for her work, about one hundred Montessori schools were opened here.

Then, almost as rapidly as it had flowered, American interest in Montessori faded away.

According to J. McV. Hunt, of the University of Illinois, the reason for this collapse was that Montessori's ideas ran head-on against several other trends that were just becoming prominent in the United States at that time—for example, the intelligence-testing movement, which assumed a fixed intelligence, and the psychoanalytic movement, which emphasized psychosexual, rather than cognitive, development. He points out that just as Montessori was making her first trip to America, the earliest studies showing evanescence of the effects of practice were coming out. They appeared to imply that teaching children reading, writing, and counting before they were about eight years old was, at best, a waste of time and, as Kilpatrick noted, might possibly be harmful. These studies later turned out to be crude and misleading, but they had left their mark.

Montessori also suffered from the antagonism of William

Heard Kilpatrick, the "million-dollar professor" at Teachers College, Columbia University, who used his interpretation of John Dewey as a weapon. "Madame Montessori hoped to remake pedagogy; but her idea of pedagogy is much narrower than is Professor Dewey's idea of education," he declared. "His conception of the nature of the thinking process, together with his doctrines of interest and of education as life—not simply a preparation for life—include all that is valid in Madame Montessori's doctrines of liberty and sense-training, afford the criteria for correcting her errors, and besides, go vastly further in the construction of the educational method."

Eloquent and persuasive, Kilpatrick almost singlehandedly ended the first Montessori boom in the United States. However, the method continued to thrive in Europe.

Its revival in America half a century later can be attributed just as singlehandedly to the activity of a voluble redhead named Nancy McCormick Rambusch. While on a fellowship at the Sorbonne, where she studied literature and philology, she had become acquainted with the French Montessori Association and was impressed with how well a "Frenchified" Montessori approach seemed to work there. After her first child was born, she decided to take a one-year Montessori training course in England; she then returned to New York and started a little play group to see whether Montessori would be applicable in the United States. She concluded that it was. Eventually, she and her husband, a designer of church interiors, moved with their two children to Connecticut. In 1958, with the backing of people she met there, including one of Ethel Kennedy's sisters, she opened a lay Catholic school run on the Montessori system—the Whitby School of Greenwich, Connecticut.

So successful was this school that other Montessori schools soon sprang up on the same model. Mrs. Rambusch then set up a teacher-training center at Whitby, started the American Montessori Society (A.M.S.), and in 1962 published her influential book *Learning How to Learn—An American Approach to Montessori*. In it, she pointed out that Montessori held the answers to many of the questions that were then troubling parents of preschool children—particularly parents who wanted their children to become free, autonomous, and ruggedly individual, rather than overly adjusted to the group.

Much of what Montessori had discovered sixty years earlier was becoming fashionable again: the ungraded primary classroom, the importance of the earliest years of life, the need to fix the child's attention. Mrs. Rambusch criticized nursery and kindergarten teachers who, when they see a child eager to begin reading at three or four, reroute him into bead-stringing and block play because they believe he is not ready to learn. Sarcastically, she wrote, "What does it merit a five-year-old to *read*, one is told, if he doesn't *jump* satisfactorily? These teachers find repugnant the notion that children actually derive pleasure from the exertion involved in what is to them 'work.' On seeing children so intent on a structured sensory-motor activity that they frown in concentration, the adult reaction is as often one of pity as of pleasure. . . . If, as Montessori has suggested, the environment 'should reveal the child and not mould him,' this real interest in academic learning at an early age deserves a sympathetic hearing on the teacher's part."

For Mrs. Rambusch, however, the Montessori method was a point of departure, not a point of arrival. She began to Americanize it by adding such activities as easel painting and clay modeling, some new educational toys in tune with the Montessori philosophy, and some modern equipment, such as tape recorders for language development. She discovered that teachers from alien cultures did not always understand American children, even though they were certified Montessori teachers, and that special American training courses might be necessary for them.

She also wanted Montessori teachers to study the New Math and linguistics, so as to gain a better understanding of Montessori practices.

These additions did not please all the Montessori enthusiasts in this country. Soon a full-blown schism developed in the Montessori movement which she had started. Adding fuel to the fire, Mrs. Rambusch published a vehement manifesto in 1963, warning that the American Montessori movement would be destroyed if it represented "the fossilized outlook of those Europeans whose fidelity to Dr. Montessori's memory is as unquestioned as is their innocence of the complexity of American culture."

The controversy rages on—much to the chagrin of Montessori teachers, who are now caught between the conflicting goals of the American Montessori Society, which followed Rambusch, and the more orthodox Association Montessori Internationale, whose American representative—trained by Montessori herself—feels that the training of A.M.S. teachers does not come up to the standards of A.M.I.

In general, the International Montessori approach tends to be much more disciplined and rigid than that of the A.M.S., though there are plenty of exceptions to prove the rule. Since Montessori's death in 1952 (the same year as John Dewey's), the defender of the faith has been her son Mario Montessori, who, from Holland, controls the source of pure Montessori equipment and wisdom.

There are also some Montessori schools that prosper as business enterprises, without affiliation with either Montessori society. My own first contact with such a Montessori school nearly soured me on the whole method because, unfortunately, it was a caricature of what Montessori had intended.

When I took my four-year-old son for a trial session in this school, he was fascinated by the strange-looking equipment and went around the room exploring it. The teacher, a rather stern

Indian woman who wore a colorful sari, seated him at a little table and gave him two tablets to feel. After awhile, Michael got up to look for more exciting fare. He picked up some blocks with symbols on them, and sat happily making trains out of them. When the teacher noticed this, she looked annoyed. Removing the blocks, she said, "We want you to do the things we suggest," and she pointed to the two tablets. "But I've done that already— I know one side's rough, the other smooth," protested my son. "We do things many times here," replied the teacher dryly. And as she passed near me, she muttered, "He has little concentration, doesn't he?" A little girl was tugging at her sleeve then. "Sit down and rub hard, and don't walk around the room," the teacher ordered her. There were some twenty children of various ages in the room, in nearly absolute quiet. One boy sat blindfolded on a red mat, feeling different fabrics to see whether he could identify them by their textures. A tiny girl was concentrating on a buttoning frame, buttoning and unbuttoning it very deftly. Michael got up again, though less confidently, and hunted for something else to do. He touched some long strings of counting beads as though he wanted to take one.

"No, you can't do that until you've done a lot of other things," said the teacher. At a loss, Michael picked up some weights and worked with them desultorily, then went to see what the others were doing. But all the children worked by themselves, ignoring him. The headmistress walked into the room, quietly. "How's the new child doing?" she asked the teacher. The teacher made a face. "He just runs from one thing to another," she replied. She then went over to Michael, who had picked up some small strings of beads, and resignedly explained to him that the idea was to match the number of beads on the string with some number cards, which she gave him; satisfied at last, he settled down to do this. A little later, the children had juice and cookies. Then they all sat in a circle, with their arms folded against their chests, and watched the teacher demonstrate the ritual use of colored pencils with geometrical insets. "I wouldn't want to stay here all day, all the time," Michael said at the end of his visit.

Nearly everything in this class violated the Montessori spirit: the restriction of movement, the insistence on quiet, the class-wide demonstration, the lack of freedom of choice, and particularly the teacher's authoritarian attitude—which probably owed more to the Indian custom of reverence for one's elders than to any method of instruction. It destroyed what J. McV. Hunt calls Montessori's major contribution, her solution of "the problem of the match": letting the child find out for himself what best matches his own particular interests and stage of development.

My next encounter with a Montessori school more than made up for this discouraging experience.

In a big room with a high ceiling and a skylight, forty-two children of various ages, from toddlers to five-year-olds, were engrossed in dozens of different occupations. One tiny girl of about three was washing carrots in a low basin; she scrubbed them with a brush, then impulsively took a lick before beginning to scrape them. Two youngsters worked at a double easel, making wild splashes of color with their paints. A young man—one of the few and much-wanted male teachers for this age group—drew a crowd of four or five children as he began to mix some Play-dough. At the blackboard, a ponytailed girl worked in fierce concentration: Right next to her, on a low table, were spread out some large sandpaper numbers; first she traced them with her finger, then stared at them carefully, then she turned to the board and wrote them out. As soon as she finished a number, she looked at the sandpaper model again to check what she had done; in a few cases she erased her own mistakes, doing each number over until she had written it perfectly. She was having trouble with number 8 when a teacher came around, so the girl asked for help.

The teacher, Mrs. Thomas Hopkins, showed the child how

to write an 8, and suggested that she fill up the rest of the board with this number. She spoke gently, in a melodious voice. Then she moved on to give another youngster some individual attention. There were four adults in the room—two teachers and two assistants—but I was hardly aware of their presence as they moved quietly from one child to the next amid the changing configurations in the room.

On a blue mat on the floor, a little Negro boy was working with a wooden jigsaw puzzle: a map of North and Central America, with the United States in orange, Canada in yellow. As though inspired by this sight, another little boy soon came near him carrying another mat, which he unrolled carefully, and a puzzle that represented South America. When the first boy finished his puzzle, he put it away neatly.

Suddenly the noise in the room changed as two little girls were heard quarreling at the blackboard. "Don't keep talking to me! You're disturbing me!" shouted one high-pitched voice. "You started it!" shouted another. From another end of the room, which was divided by low bookshelves into separate work areas, Mrs. Hopkins tinkled a little bell. "One child told me today it's a bit too noisy," she said politely, "so will you try and be a little more quiet—speak in softer voices for awhile?" The children complied, keeping their noise more subdued.

Several tables had room for more than one child. At one larger, round table a boy was polishing his shoes with liquid shoe polish; a girl was working with solid cones, cubes, and egg shapes; a very small boy was handling two-dimensional versions of the same shapes, obviously for the first time, and next to him a teacher was demonstrating what he could do with them. Undistracted by any of these activities, another girl at the same table had traced a circle with a metal inset and was busy filling it with parallel lines.

This was the West Side Montessori School of New York, begun by a group of parents in 1963 and directed by Mrs. Hopkins. She had studied Montessori techniques in England and taught in English and French Montessori schools before being invited to the United States by Nancy Rambusch. After teaching at Whitby for awhile, she opened a Montessori school in Altoona, Pennsylvania—the first private school in that town. The school started with only thirty students but now has about one hundred eighty, with teachers imported from Holland and England. "In 1961, there had been few articles about Montessori except in Catholic magazines, so we really had to fight to get in all three religions," recalls Mrs. Hopkins. As at Whitby, the parents became so enthusiastic about the school that they did not wish to take their children out at the end of the kindergarten year, but kept adding one grade each year, so that their children could continue learning the Montessori way. The West Side Montessori School is run along similar lines, but because of the many schools available in New York City it does not go beyond the preschool years.

There is a fantastic difference between the behavior of European and American children in Montessori schools, according to Mrs. Hopkins. Being more disciplined at home, the European children are much quieter and have more fear of adults; they have been told what to do so often that they see the little rules rather than the big ones, and sometimes won't do anything at all until they know whether it is right. Therefore the Montessori teacher has to develop their independence.

American children, on the other hand, come from child-centered homes; as a result, they have plenty of independence, and much more vitality. "Montessori is *especially* well adapted to American children," Mrs. Hopkins declares. "You can give them big rules, and within these they can act—go as fast or as slow as they wish. They have the initiative, and they'll go. But it won't be a quiet classroom! I've had to change my attitude towards quiet, motion, and socialization. These children interact, so it can't be quiet—it wouldn't be natural for them. We must be more liberal than the Europeans."

When children start school in the fall, they start with a very small group, and the room it quite empty, she explained. Gradually, more equipment is brought out, and more children come in. After a few months, they know how to control the classroom. They know the limits, so they're free.

I visited the school again one year later. Its layout had changed somewhat, because of a situation not uncommon in parent-run schools: an influx of younger siblings. It seemed that when all the children gathered together in a single room, the big sibs drove the little sibs wild by trying to do everything for them, robbing them of their initiative. As one mother put it, the older ones made the little ones absolutely green. The little ones didn't really bother their big brothers or sisters. This was further complicated by the presence of some of the teachers' own children, who clamored for special attention. As a temporary solution, the class was finally split into two groups of twenty-two children each, according to age, with one teacher and one assistant teacher per group, plus the part-time attention of the precious male instructor. The ages were to be mixed again, though in two classes, the following year. The older group stuck longer with their chosen tasks. They received a great deal of individual attention. The teacher would spend as much as ten minutes with a child if she felt there was something important to demonstrate; during such periods the child would talk to her in a very concentrated way, getting more practice in speech than he might get in many kindergartens that stress general conversation.

At one time I saw Mrs. Hopkins deeply involved, for a span of twenty minutes, with three little boys to whom she explained the operation of the Bank game. She used sets of small golden beads, with which the children were already familiar, and showed them how, when they had gathered ten single beads, they could go to the "bank," on a shelf, and exchange them for a ten-bar. When they had ten ten-bars, they had one hundred—a perfect square, or one side of a cube. When they had ten hundreds, they had one thousand—the whole cube. The boys seemed fascinated by this revelation of the decimal system.

A little girl was sitting alone and writing her own words and sentences on lined paper. Next to her stood a box full of small, colored paper shapes. Mrs. Hopkins joined her for a while and explained how these could be used to color-code each part of a sentence: The shiny red circles should be pasted under the verbs, she said; the small black triangles represented adjectives; the large blue triangles represented nouns. The little girl had written, "I can run fast." As Mrs. Hopkins watched, the child pasted a red circle under the word "run." Then she began to write other verbs, so as to paste more circles: "skip, hop, jump, clap." Next she wrote "yellow," and carefully pasted a small triangle. It looked as if she would never stop.

Of all the children I could see in the room, the most mysteriously occupied was a little girl who kept leaving her table and running to the "bank," then filling little pieces of paper with columns of numbers labeled "B F L U." I could not figure out what they meant. One of the papers went like this:

$$
\begin{array}{cccc}
B & F & L & U \\
1 & 2 & 3 & 4 \\
+ & 5 & 4 & 5 \\
\hline
2 & 2 & 2 & 3 \\
\end{array}
$$

Obviously, this child cannot add, I thought. But then, why did she seem so sure of herself, and so engrossed in what she was doing? At an opportune moment I asked Mrs. Hopkins to explain. "She's adding up numbers on the basis of 6," said Mrs. Hopkins, as though this were the most natural thing in the world for a little girl who, it turned out, was not yet five years old. "She uses special cubes, squares, and single strands of six beads each, as well as individual beads, so she can add them up physically first. She takes what she needs from the bank, and then writes down the result." The mysterious letters that headed the columns of figures were there for her guidance, Mrs. Hopkins added. "B" stood for "blocks" of 216 beads; "F" for "flat," 36-bead squares; "L" for "long" strands of six beads each; and "U" for single "units." An example of outside materials that can be fitted into the Montessori environment, these cubes and beads were developed by a contemporary Hungarian mathematician, Z. P. Dienes.

"Some of the children can add and subtract even at the age of four," said Mrs. Hopkins. "They can do it as soon as they learn and understand the numbers one to ten, since we show them different ways of making up these numbers. It all depends on the child's interest. In this group, they seem more interested in numbers work than in letters. It's more materialized, more physical and encouraging. They can't just pick up a book and read, so that's more frustrating, especially if they have been pushed too much at home. I think the parents push letters more than math, so we're more successful with numbers!"

Just as sad as the pushing parents, she added, were those who said, "We don't teach our children anything at home—we don't believe in it." Both showed a misunderstanding of what was important. "The school does try to explain to parents what's going to happen here," she pointed out. "Some of the children will read, some won't. It isn't what they've learned as such that counts; it's the ability to learn. This is the hardest thing to get across, because the newspapers have generally given the impression that knowledge and reading skills are everything."

The children's occupations are never the same from day to day. "It goes in waves," commented Mrs. Hopkins. One week they like bank games best, another week it's sensorial work, such as "wet games." Some observers were absolutely horrified one day to find the children spending most of their time washing the floor with mops, and one woman exclaimed, "My goodness, don't they ever do anything else?"

Montessori teachers generally try to avoid admitting older children into their classes for the first time, on the theory that by then certain critical periods have passed. "If you take them as late as four or five, you can never interest them in sandpaper letters or sensorial materials," Mrs. Hopkins explained. "They just won't want to sit there and match two red tablets. So they will have lost much of the foundations."

I looked into the younger children's room to find out how they were getting these foundations. Most prominent was a fat white rabbit in a cage, eating a carrot as a little boy watched. One little girl was solemnly shining her shoes. Another one sat on the floor, on a mat, and arranged blue and red counting rods of graduated lengths. In one corner of the room, three little girls sat looking at picture books. A small girl was sponging off a big blackboard. A boy was putting the correct number of sticks into a box with compartments labeled for each number from zero to ten; the teacher had just started him off, and he continued contentedly.

Passing by the carrot stand, one boy picked up some of the remaining carrot peelings and fed them to the rabbit. This seemed to give another boy an idea; he carefully peeled a fresh carrot and offered it to the rabbit, leaving the peelings behind. As the rabbit munched his clean carrot, a little girl walked by the washbasin, saw the peels, and promptly ate them. Nobody interfered: Montessori teachers try to avoid correcting children's mistakes, Mrs. Hopkins explained later. When a child misunderstands the purpose of an exercise, the teacher simply notes the need to repeat her demonstration of it.

After a while, one of the teachers began to read a book, in a low voice, to three of the children. Skipping along, a little blonde girl in a ponytail put all her number rods away in the proper place, then joined the story group. When most of the children had gathered around her, the teacher asked the rest of them, each by name, to put away their work and join her. Then she announced, "I'm going to let the rabbit out, because he needs exercise—but don't move, so as not to frighten him." The children were delighted. Once freed, the rabbit began jumping about. The children sang some standard nursery songs, such as "Shoofly," but kept an eye on the rabbit, who suddenly came and nuzzled one little girl's ear.

"There's a lot more interaction with the teacher than I had expected," commented a visiting kindergarten teacher, who was watching all this. "I thought they'd rely more on the equipment to teach."

Another visiting teacher remarked that she didn't like the teachers' relationship with the children. "It isn't warm enough," she said. When I asked Mrs. Hopkins about this comment, she replied, "I'm not about to cuddle anybody, hug them, or pick them up—especially not five-year-olds, who resent physical contact and demand the same kind of respect they give us. A child wants to be treated as a person, an independent being. We had a trainee here who tried to hug them all the time—they really hated it. Any physical control of the child is bad. I just talk to them, and it works. There is too much mothering in the average American nursery school. A teacher is somebody quite different from a parent."

The debate over Montessori continues after each meeting held for prospective parents. I attended one such meeting to find out what questions would be asked, and what answers given. The evening began with a short speech by Mrs. L. F. Boker Doyle, one of the founders of the school and president of its board of trustees. Then Mrs. Hopkins took over. "First, I'd like to tell you what our day is like," she started, somewhat diffidently. "The first hour of the day is perhaps comparable to other nursery schools' free play. The children can work at whatever they like. They can take anything from anywhere and work with it. The only restriction is not to disturb others. If a child is a nuisance, he may be asked to leave.

"When they get noisy and wiggly, and are really not enjoying it anymore, we go outside. Then, when they come back, different groups have art, music, or language games—such as find the nouns, the adjectives, the verbs—or poems and songs. It's guided by the child's desire." She then ran through various sets of Montessori equipment, describing their uses. "We explain the equipment to the child at the beginning," she said. "He gets so he can do it blindfolded; he knows these things. So if he does it some other way it's just because he thinks it's funny, because he's found another way to do it. And we *don't* stop him."

First question from the floor: "How does what a child learns here affect him when he goes to elementary school?"

"We hope it improves him," replied Mrs. Doyle instantly. "But there is one situation our admission committee is terrified of: the parent who feels a Montessori education is a one-way ticket to Harvard. We want the child to come here and enjoy his three years. We're not in the business of force-feeding learning to children—we simply make the equipment for learning available. So don't expect them to go away knowing calculus and algebra, or reading Shakespeare."

A woman in the audience asked what happened when a child did not, by himself, get involved with the equipment. Mrs. Hopkins noted that when this happened, "usually the parents have been too pushing. If one is pushed too much, or feels one can't do all that is expected, the safest thing is not to try. So first we try to find out what's going on and why. In school we may just leave the child alone for three weeks. Let him walk around and see what the others are doing. It's all very relaxed—there's no pressure, and no achievement is demanded or expected of him. The only thing we require is, he may not upset everything and disturb others."

Don't you use the usual equipment, such as trains, dolls, and blocks? asked one parent. "There is a certain amount we omit because we feel it's usually available at home," answered Mrs. Doyle. "We feel it's not worth while having a nursery school that reproduces the homes of one group of children. We do have blocks, but a bit less ambiguous ones—a tower built out of cones is different."

"What is your approach to art?" somebody else wanted to know. There was some defensiveness in Mrs. Doyle's voice as she replied, "We have a teacher here, Mr. Savoye, with a degree in fine arts." And he took over the floor. "All I do is vary the mediums they can use—clay, paint," he said. "Montessori herself, I think, was not very artistically oriented. She was a product of her time in esthetics. But she really produces a very competent individual, which is the best background for an artist. There isn't any conflict in my mind between Montessori and creativity."

"What achievements, by a typical child, can you point to?" asked one mother. Mrs. Doyle's reply was rather foxy: "A few came in very quiet and timid, and didn't talk," she said, sounding for all the world like any conventional nursery-school teacher. "Now they are more outgoing and can socialize. They like to play, they like to work. They're more confident. They can *choose* something to do—or if they don't do anything, that's okay too. But a few others still can't do anything without checking first to see what the other children are doing." Not a word about the three Rs, which this question was obviously about.

Trying a different tack, a woman then asked about the major differences between this school and other nursery schools. Here Mrs. Doyle did not hestitate. "First, we stress reality over fantasy life," she said. "The typical progressive school tends to stress fantasy play over reality.

"Second, there is individual instruction rather than group work. We do not have the teacher at the center of the classroom. In other schools, when the teacher says 'We sing now,' we sing—every one of us!

"Third, academic material is available, whereas in ninety percent of the preschools in this country, there is no academic material. They say that the kids learn to read when they recognize their names, or that they learn science when they bring in an icicle and see that it melts [laughter from the audience]. We all agree that learning can go much beyond that. The tools with which to learn, and become familiar with learning and confident about it, are here. That's why Montessori is exploding around the country. The child is given the opportunity to move from the physical world he's used to, where he handles things, to the abstract, like alphabet, numbers. He learns because he has related the two.

"Our emphasis is not so much on social adjustment. Yet I would not go so far as to say there is no opportunity for it."

From the point of view of education for the children of poverty, the Montessori method has at least one extraordinary asset: its peculiar ability to increase the child's span of attention.

Reporting on a Montessori program that included ten Negro children from families receiving Aid to Dependent Children (ADC) in Chicago, Professor Lawrence Kohlberg, of the University of Chicago's psychology department, noted that an obvious fact about the disadvantaged is their defect in attention, due to an environment of constant distractions. They are never alone with any task. At home, their brothers and sisters pounce upon any object they may be trying to play with. The conventional progressive-permissive approach increases these tendencies. But in a Montessori class, he pointed out, the children show long periods of attention, since they are not disturbed. Such attention is easiest to promote in a nongroup context. The preschool years offer a unique opportunity for this kind of solitary, self-directed work.

The IQ's of the ten disadvantaged children jumped an average of 17 points after only three months in the Montessori program, Kohlberg declared, while the IQ's of the same group's middle-class children increased about 10 points. "In our view," he said, "Montessori is useful not for sensory education as such, but for its ordering and labeling activities. However, the sensory activities are pleasurable, and serve as a basis for the development of attention."

Kohlberg also reported on a summer Head Start program run by the same Montessori teacher in the same way. Probably because of its short duration, the children in this group showed no significant changes.

Elsewhere in Chicago, in the city's oldest public-housing project—a nineteen-story development once described as a high-rise slum for low-income Negroes—another Montessori school for disadvantaged children is being run by a young woman named Marcella Morrison.

The whole atmosphere of Cabrini Houses is one of tremendous depression, says Miss Morrison, who was trained at Whitby. It weighs very heavily on the children—almost like being stifled. For instance, there is never anyone at the playground. Thousands of people live in the development, but, except at noon, when children are being dismissed from school, they all stay at home—the world is too threatening. There is no social contact. The Montessori school is the highlight of these children's lives. They begin to find life interesting, and they want to come to terms with it, to get involved.

When they started school, they had almost no span of attention, she recalls. It was bedlam. They were screaming and pushing all the time. Many teachers get stuck right at that spot, and never progress, on the theory that "that's the way they are," she says. Or else teachers become so strict that there is no spontaneity, gaiety, spark, left in the kids; the children conform and just seem to die out. With Montessori, they are not stuck at any one step. Provide an atmosphere that's rich in possibilities—and things really do happen. Although she knows they happen, Miss Morrison has not yet had the opportunity to test the children's progress. She hopes to do so if the OEO provides the money.

As Maria Montessori ran her original school, it was a day-care center, and lasted the whole day. There was time, therefore, for free play, for conversation, for taking care of pets, and for a lot of activities that she did not fully spell out, since they were not too unusual. In her daily program for the first Casa dei Bambini, she allowed only one hour for "intellectual work" with the equipment generally thought of as typically Montessori.

When the program is limited to a half-day, however, the problem of selection becomes more severe. This is especially true in planning for underprivileged youngsters who may have few opportunities to talk or play at home. While the prepared environment leaves little to chance—it was meant that way—it also limits the child's opportunity to make something uniquely his own, except in writing. All the equipment seems to bear the message "There is only one way of doing things—and this is it."

J. McV. Hunt believes that Montessori's materials should be viewed as a beginning, to which modern minds can add many useful inventions. As an example, he cites the work of O. K. Moore.

Clearly, Moore owes much to Montessori in his responsive environments method. Moore himself feels that his approach is essentially different, however, because unlike his talking typewriter, Montessori's materials cannot respond. The Montessori scheme is noninteractional, he told me. The child can't change the Montessori materials; he must adjust to them.

Since the Montessori method remained popular in Europe throughout the half-century when it was forgotten in the United States, I was very interested to hear Jean Piaget's comments about it. Piaget sees Montessori in the stream of educational reformers that includes such progressives as John Dewey and Carleton Washburne. The school with which he is associated in Geneva uses many elements of the Montessori system, he says, but in a more flexible way. The main drawback of the orthodox Montessori schools is that their equipment never changes—it was given once and for all, Piaget points out. He believes there are lots of good ideas there, but equipment should be changed according to need, as one goes along. Those famous weights, for example, are just one type of seriation; one could prepare twenty others along the same lines, using anything at all. He also criticizes Montessori's method on the ground that it provides only fragments of activity, without enabling the child truly to create anything. However, he admits, the Montessori system does promote continuity of effort and a passion for learning.

This half-century of experience in many parts of the world also shows, according to Nancy Rambusch, that the Montessori method is generally benign. At the very least, it doesn't seem to do any harm. One famous graduate was Anne Frank, whose youthful diary showed no signs of stunted creativity.

Mrs. Rambusch has been experimenting with one-hour Montessori classes for youngsters in run-down neighborhoods. Since an early start is particularly important for these children, and Montessori showed how to focus the interests of children as young as two and a half, the method holds great promise for them. Even in 1907, points out Mrs. Rambusch, Montessori worked with children from the age of two and a half years, at a time when American educators were discussing the relevance of her ideas for the four- and five-year-olds in public school kindergartens.

Another advantage of the Montessori system is its reasonable cost. Montessori's first directress was a teen-age girl, the daughter of the superintendent of the housing project in which Montessori established her first Casa dei Bambini. Almost singlehandedly, this girl directed the learning of fifty to sixty children, ranging in age from three to seven. Although this ratio of pupils to teacher seems excessively high, and Montessori teachers must now undergo considerable training, the method certainly requires less personnel than do many of the new techniques. Its equipment, too, is relatively inexpensive.

All this points to the likelihood that the Montessori revival in the United States will continue. The method may become further modified, or Americanized. It may return, at last, to the slums for which it was originally designed. But on its second transplanting, its roots seem to have taken firm hold.

Chapter 7

OTHER ATTEMPTS TO

HALT THE DOWNWARD

SPIRAL

SEVERAL less radical innovators than either Bereiter, Moore, or the new Montessorians—and therefore more acceptable to the average school board—have been trying, ever since 1962, to work out new programs for culturally disadvantaged preschoolers, with varying results.

Some, like the influential team in New York's Institute for Developmental Studies, have started out with few preconceived ideas about curriculum and gradually developed their own techniques, which are still in a state of flux. Others, like Dr. Susan Gray, in Nashville, Tennessee, antedated the summer Head Start idea by several years and greatly superseded it in the thoroughness of their research and planning. Still others, like Dr. David Weikart, of Ypsilanti, Michigan, suffered the slings and arrows of the "second-year slump"—a constant threat to researchers who are conscientious enough to use proper control groups. In some ways they follow the tracks of earlier experimenters in Israel, where the problem of disadvantaged children is far more acute.

Dr. Martin Deutsch, director of the Institute for Developmental Studies, is probably the best-known figure in this group. One of the first American psychologists to see the need for special preschool programs for poor children and to fight for them, Deutsch now has his finger in nearly every pie that bears this label. His staff of more than a hundred psychologists, teachers, social workers, and consultants runs dozens of studies, trains scores of teachers, takes part in countless seminars and workshops, consults with school officials all over the country, is deluged by observers from all over the world, and publishes a torrent of papers. It is the recipient of grants from numerous foundations, as well as from the New York City Board of Education. In sheer size, it towers above all the other enterprises in this field.

The institute's major effort is a long-term program of special classes for slum children within the public schools. These classes go on for a period of five years—from age four, or prekindergarten, right on to the end of third grade. About 350 children, mostly Negroes and Puerto Ricans, are enrolled in various stages of this operation, from which they will emerge in waves, beginning in June, 1967.

Having established, through a series of studies, that slum children differ from middle-class children in specific ways—narrower range of language, lack of attention, poor auditory discrimination, and the like—Deutsch set out to give his pupils the kind of stimulation and enrichment that would better prepare them for school. However, he did not want to introduce any revolutionary changes. Starting with a regular nursery program, his goal was to systematize the methods employed by good teachers, and also to develop some new educational materials. The best teachers often cannot identify their best techniques, he said, explaining that he planned to identify what worked best, and in what sequences. The teachers whose aid he enlisted in this way became increasingly self-observant and effective. But the first classes that resulted were not too different from ordinary nursery schools, except for their clientele and their aims.

It soon became clear that even systematized enrichment was not enough, and that simple increases in content, such as vocabulary, do not necessarily imply improvement in more abstract and conceptual functions, as Deutsch's wife, Dr. Cynthia Deutsch, a psychologist, noted recently. The first level of research has shown the possibility of arresting or retarding the accumulation of deficit, she declared. The task now is to refine the new techniques so that disadvantaged children can substantially overlap middle-class norms.

This refinement of techniques has led the institute team to realize that young children can learn much more than it had ever anticipated. In fact, the institute can hardly keep up with them.

"More and more, we find that very little is learned in a group situation. So we break up the class into smaller and smaller groups, until it is nearly individualized," explained Caroline Saxe, who showed me around some of the latest-model kindergarten classes run by the institute.

At P.S. 79, in East Harlem, we passed by several ordinary classrooms in which rows upon rows of children sat listening to a single teacher, or staring into space. The walls of these rooms were often cluttered with various posters up to the ceiling. We also passed one of the institute's prekindergarten classes, which happened to be empty that day, as the children were out on a field trip. It was an oasis of order and clarity. "We pay a lot of attention to the layout of each classroom," said Mrs. Saxe as we stepped into this room. "We ask the teacher to get down on her hands and knees to see things from the child's eye level. We want everything to be neat and easy to focus on, so the child is not put off by overcrowded or distracting displays." The room was divided into several harmonious sections. On a low bookshelf, within easy reach for a small child, Mrs. Saxe showed me a series of related objects: a large picture of farm animals, tractors, and other equipment; some rubber animals of the same type for the child to handle; and a book that told a story about a boy on a farm.

Nearby stood a capital-letter Alphabet Board, one of the institute's new devices. This consists of 3-inch-high letters, which must be fitted into appropriate slots on a board, making a puzzle out of the alphabet. Another innovation was Language Lotto, designed by Dr. Lassar G. Gotkin, a senior research associate. Instead of teaching vocabulary, this teaches such concepts as "on" and "under" by means of cards that picture specific relationships. The teacher may ask, for example, "Who has the blocks *in* the box?" and the child who has the right card must answer in a full sentence. Everything in the room had its purpose and its place. Blocks of various sizes were arranged so as to make clear that two of one kind equalled one of the next. Many of the toys were sequenced according to size or shape.

In one corner, several wooden partitions further subdivided the area into four little nooks. Equipped with individual sets of headphones, this was the Listening Center—an interesting way of holding a modern child's attention and ensuring his privacy. Four children at one time could operate their ends of the center, hooked into a tape recorder. They could hear a story being read through their headphones, and simultaneously look at the book it was taken from, as often as they wished. Similar listening centers were used in the kindergarten classes as a form of programmed instruction.

As we entered the adjoining kindergarten room, we were greeted by a sprightly teacher, Mrs. Charlotte Glick. The children were divided into two small groups, one sitting around a long table, another clustered around a board with magnetic letters. The first group seemed less advanced. Returning to them, Mrs. Glick said, "We're going to start a new sound today." She then held up a picture of the sun, with a large "S" in its center.

"What sound does the word 'sun' start with? Ssss—that's right. As in what word?" A young voice said, "Zebra." "No, not quite," replied Mrs. Glick, and demonstrated the difference in sound. "Can you think of another word?" She continued discussing the initial letters of common words, such as "telephone" and "scissors." Each child had before him a copy of the Stern Structural Reading booklets, preparatory level.

Meanwhile, five children in the more advanced group were trying to change the beginnings of words, with the aid of a young assistant teacher. Using magnetic, lower-case letters, she had printed "batman" on the board. The children volunteered to change this to "catman" and "fatman," and put up the appropriate letters. Next, she printed the word "robin," with the children prompting her about the initial letter. Knowing what she had written, the children could then "read" the whole word. But they could not read the "bin" and "in" syllables when she hid the first part of the word from them.

In the preceding year, this class had become familiar with the shapes of upper-case letters through the Alphabet Board. A different form of the Alphabet Board, with lower-case letters, was theirs to play with this year. Now the teachers were trying to teach the sounds of these letters and explain that they made up words. Each child had his own folder, with all the lower-case letters he needed to print his own name. On the walls, several papers showed that the children had written their own names in pencil, in lower-case letters.

The entire work period took about half an hour. "I don't like to overdo it," explained Mrs. Glick. "Better to do just a little bit each day, or else their playtime gets shortened." After play and the children's snacks, they would have an hour for storytelling, the Listening Center and rhythms, and also some practice with their handwriting books, she added, pointing to an experimental edition of B. F. Skinner's *Handwriting with Write and See* (Book 1, part B).

Mrs. Glick had taught in the city school system long enough to know when she was well off. In her new role, she had an assistant teacher and, as it happened, only thirteen pupils, since this was a transient area. "The main thing is the small class and the two teachers," she commented. "You can only work well with a few children at a time. I train them to work individually, which I couldn't do when I was alone, with twenty-five children in the morning and twenty-five in the afternoon—actually, I sometimes had up to forty children in one class—and also had to service the whole building with equipment, since there were no school aides at that time. I was responsible for arts and crafts for the whole school, which meant I had to unpack and distribute all the equipment.

"Before, I taught in a whole group—and those that learned, learned, and those that didn't, didn't," she summarized. "Here, I know what they know and what they don't know. In the other setup, it was hopeless. Even when I knew, I didn't have the time to take them separately and work with them.

"Now I try to go with them as far as they can go, as long as they know what I'm talking about. If they get it, I go on to the next higher level."

A little boy began to dance an uninhibited Watusi while she talked to me. Others were working on jigsaw puzzles, or with blocks. All of them can read time—at least the hour and the half-hour, asserted Mrs. Glick. They know when it's time for milk; this brought meaning to the clock, and so now they have a concept of what time is. When she rang a little bell to announce clean-up time, the children became quiet immediately. There was a strong sense of discipline. One little girl calmly picked out thirteen straws for the children's juice. All of them helped to clean up or to prepare for the snack. They looked quite happy—a satisfied, busy, playful group, still largely focused on their teacher.

Another institute kindergarten class, run by Mrs. Edna Barnett in the heart of Harlem, seemed to have gone even further toward individualized instruction. Early one morning, four of the twenty-one children in this class were directed to the Listening Center by an assistant teacher, who said, "You'll take your crayons and do what the voice tells you to do, won't you?" Facing away from the rest of the class, separated from one another by wooden partitions, the children sat down in their little cubicles and adjusted their headphones, which looked like giant earmuffs. Then, following instructions from the tape recorder, they selected crayons of various colors and underlined designated objects in their mimeographed booklets.

In a different part of the room, three girls were playing numbers lotto. One called the numbers, the other two played against each other. A little boy came up to Mrs. Barnett, who hugged him. "Do you want to play with words or with numbers?" she asked him. "Words!" said the little boy. "All right, then go over to the board there and play with Sally." The two children wandered off to the blackboard, to chalk up "bat" and "cat." Another small group played with numbers, guided by the assistant teacher, while at a farther table one girl was helping a little boy recognize numerals. Sitting alone, another little girl scribbled in a workbook; she turned the page and silently read a question, then wrote out her reply, "It is on the chick," in large, lower-case letters. (Later, Mrs. Barnett explained that this child was up to second grade in reading, largely because of tutoring at home from an older sister who had been in the same program two years earlier.)

This was quiet-work time—a rediscovery of the obvious, perhaps, but a genuine innovation for teachers trained in early-child-hood education. It had started quite spontaneously in this room at the beginning of the year, as a few minutes during which children could work freely with materials leading up to the skills needed in first grade. Unlike the conventional early-childhood "work time," it did not include play with trucks or blocks.

Only a few minutes long at first, the quiet-work time now lasts at least one hour. As in the Montessori method, it first captured the children's attention with puzzles and manipulative materials, then moved on to symbols. But many of the activities remain centered on the teacher.

Mrs. Barnett wrote a list of words on the blackboard: *pot, cot, hot, tot, lot, dot.* "I'd like someone to put a line under the word that says 'hot,' " she suggested to half a dozen children who had cluttered around her. A little boy did it. "Who'll put a circle around the word that says 'pot'?" she continued. The children enjoyed the double challenge of finding the right word and doing the right thing to it. They laughed and seemed very excited at the game. In another part of the room, a similar game was going on with numbers, with one of the children acting as teacher and trying to invent difficult things for the others to do. Meanwhile, four different children were called by the assistant teacher to take their turns at the Listening Center.

"It used to be discouraged, all this cognitive work," recalled Mrs. Barnett, who had been a kindergarten teacher for ten years before joining the institute group. "They said we shouldn't bother the child. They said the children's eyes weren't strong enough, and that all we should work on was social skills—how to get along together. But there's no reason why you can't have a game that also teaches them letters or numbers. For them, it's a game! And now they're independent enough to work in small groups or by themselves. I think they're wonderful! At the beginning of the year, I was very discouraged, but suddenly it all began to fall into place. Some of them are quite advanced now. With others, we can't understand what the problem is."

The quiet-work time was followed by snack time and play time —painting, dress-up corner, block-building, arts and crafts, games. The two teachers wandered about from group to group, encouraging conversation in the housekeeping corner, passing out advice or colored paper and scissors. This took about half an hour. Then came clean-up time, story time, and time for rhythms.

It struck me that these children acted very much like average middle-class youngsters. They had adopted all the standard games and toys, and had much of the same ease. But Gotkin pointed out that this was the result of deliberate training. When these children played with games that are found in many middle-class homes, such as Chutes and Ladders, which require a good knowledge of numbers and a willingness to follow rules, "we had to *teach* them to play these games," he said. "What you see is the end result."

Unlike conventional kindergartens, where one can't see much change in the program over time, the curriculum worked out by Gotkin together with Mrs. Fay Fondiller tries to keep the children moving on from one step to the next, in logical sequences. "Now we're going to teach them to play questioning games," said Gotkin. He hoped this would develop their spirit of inquiry and their ability to ask fruitful questions.

"Our biggest problem is that we're running out of curriculum," he added. "We didn't plan originally, last year, to teach them words. We were going to give them just the beginning of phonics, to make them ready to learn. But if you individualize instruction, some of the kids—maybe forty percent—move so quickly, once they break the code, that they run out of material. So we've started to put letters together, to combine them, rather than teach all the sounds first. One of the teachers started this as a game last year, and we've adopted it for all our kindergarten classes this year."

In summary, there is nothing very extraordinary about these classes—except the fact that they actually do what one would expect of them. Reviewing the nation's programs of compensatory education before members of the American Association for the Advancement of Science, psychologist Edmond W. Gordon, of Yeshiva University, marveled at their lack of really new or radical innovations. "Most of the programs use common-sense procedures which are, or should be, part of any good educational program," he said. "It is, in fact, something of an indictment that we have not introduced these practices earlier."

The institute represents one of the best efforts of this essentially conservative approach. Its kindergarten classes are effective because the teachers can work with small groups of children, and because they have specific goals. They also benefit from close supervision by curriculum specialists. Each afternoon the teachers take time to meet, compare notes, evaluate changes in procedures, and think out the next steps in the program. All this makes for an expensive operation (it costs about $1,500 per child per year, excluding the research), and when other groups try to imitate it, the chief danger is the temptation to water it down to ineffectiveness.

Only the cream of the crop of the culturally disadvantaged take part in these classes, since the institute expects parents to provide their own transportation, and the parents had to know enough to apply for admission to the program in the first place. Furthermore, the institute kept out all children who did not speak English, who were obviously mentally retarded, or who were seriously disturbed. All the children lived in overpopulated slum areas, however, and about a third of the families were on welfare.

The mean IQ of the first group that applied was 99 on the Stanford-Binet—pretty high for slum children. On a random basis, two-thirds of these children were then put into the enriched pre-kindergartens, while the others served as self-selected controls. Another group of children from similar backgrounds, but whose parents had not applied to the institute, served as additional controls. None of the control children was given any prekindergarten experience, though both groups were to attend regular kindergartens.

A third group of children tested by the institute consisted of youngsters whose parents did not enroll them in any of the city's public kindergartens, which are optional, at age five. These entered school for the first time at age six, at first grade, and they consistently scored lower than any of the other three groups at the same age. Their low IQ's, fluctuating between 81 and 85, can be attributed either to their lack of early schooling, or to the fact that their parents made up the real, hard-core poverty cases—the multiproblem families who have lost all hope and all initiative.

By way of statistics, the institute program has little to show so far but effort. Although the children in the enriched classes have obviously changed—most of them when they came in hardly spoke at all—not much can be said about their progress in statistical terms. To begin with, the Stanford-Binet test may not be precise enough to detect what the children have learned. The same applies to other tests used by the institute, such as the Peabody Picture Vocabulary Test and the Columbia Mental Maturity Scale, whose results do not always correspond to the IQ scores. Another problem has been holding on to the children in the original classes or control groups: Many dropped out because their parents moved away, and nobody knows whether these were the most or the least capable in their groups. The program itself changed so much as it went along that the first two waves of children were, in a sense, guinea pigs. Though their IQ's rose slightly after prekindergarten and kindergarten, these results are not considered statistically significant. Only preliminary results are available about the following waves.

"This is a longitudinal study. We are not too interested in short-term results, but in the effects at fourth grade and higher," emphasizes Dr. Leo S. Goldstein, the psychologist in charge of evaluating the institute's program. He remains optimistic that at the end of the longer period of time, particularly for groups that followed the first two, these children will be performing at a level significantly better than that of their peers who have not had the enriched program—and close to the level of children from the middle socioeconomic group.

Meanwhile, the institute has been trying out other techniques on different groups of children. For example, Gotkin has been developing a sequence of lessons on the E.R.E. machine so different in spirit from Moore's approach that one would hardly know it is the same machine. He does not let the children explore the E.R.E.; he does not use their own words or ideas as a basis for individualized programs; nor does he let them take the initiative. His main concern is parsimony—providing the quickest possible preparation for reading for the largest number of children. His subjects are five-year-olds with no knowledge of the alphabet.

An early set of twenty-one lessons he developed, lasting about ten minutes each and identical for each child, starts out with a modified keyboard (on which only three letters are showing) and a lilting voice, which says, "Hello, we're going to play some games with letters." Then the voice explains, "I'm going to show you one of my letters. You find one just like mine and then press it. Are you ready?" The goal of the lessons is to cut down irrelevant behavior: they give the child clear directions and tell him exactly what to do. At the end of the three and a half hours with the E.R.E. the child should know nine letter names (six more letters are added later), plus the fact that letters go from left to right, and, hopefully, have developed an "attentional learning set" which makes him listen to instructions and search for letters visually. The regular classroom teacher then reaps the benefits of this standardized preparation.

Many observers crowd the room where the institute demonstrates its work with two E.R.E. machines once a week. On a recent Wednesday I watched, through a one-way mirror, as a little boy sat down at the keyboard. He had been there several times before.

"Keep trying to find the letter the pointer will stop on," said the machine in a sing-song voice. "Get ready—here we go-o!" When the boy pressed the right letter, the voice said, "Good!" or "That's right!" or "Very good!" And after awhile it said, ingratiatingly, "That's all for today. It was fun playing with you!"

Gotkin believes that praise is important to these children, and also that programmers should seek to be as skillful in implementing their ideas as was Walt Disney, who knew how to utilize whimsical characters and interesting voices.

The Institute for Developmental Studies keeps growing. Some of its critics feel it is spreading itself too thin. Founded in 1958, it was part of the New York Medical College for eight years, but recently moved to New York University's School of Education, where Deutsch is now professor of early childhood and elementary education. As one of the pioneers in calling attention to the preschool needs of disadvantaged children, Deutsch is baffled by the headlong rush and lack of planning which followed. "It's just as if none of the experimental work had ever existed," he comments ruefully. "Head Start could have been done very much better."

A cheaper, more limited program than Deutsch's was tried, almost simultaneously, in Tennessee. It started seven years before Head Start, when a group of psychologists from the George

Peabody College for Teachers in Nashville tried a summer pre-school program to counteract the progressive retardation they had seen among Negro children in Murfreesboro. This seemed to work, but by the end of the first grade the results had all washed out—no difference remained between the special group and the controls.

Bravely, the group decided to try a string of summers rather than a single one, and to add a weekly visit to the children's homes all year round as a link between one summer and the next. The purpose of using the summer was, of course, that school space and staff were much more easily available then, and also that a ten-week program is cheaper than one lasting a full year.

The first summer preschool in this series began in 1962, with twenty three-year-olds from poor families in which there was an average of five children. In half the cases, the fathers were absent. The children's mean IQ was 86.

Daily lesson plans were worked out for each child. Although the equipment was the same as that of conventional nursery schools, it was used in a much more deliberate manner, explains Dr. Susan Gray, the psychologist who directed the Early Training Project. For example, one-inch colored cubes served to teach numbers, colors, and position words ("Put the red block on the blue one") as well as to develop the children's drive for achievement ("Build the tallest tower you possibly can"). With only five children per adult, immediate rewards were possible.

After three summers of training, the children gained 9 points of IQ. During the same time, the control children lost 6 points. On a preschool test given to all children who entered the first grade, those who had been in the program scored nearly as well as middle-class children.

Then Dr. Gray noted a strange thing: By the end of the first grade, the controls were doing so well they nearly caught up with the experimental group, even though the latter had retained their

gains in IQ. However, another control group in a town sixty miles
away did not show the same progress. This led her to assume that
the local children's gain must have resulted from diffusion—from
the influence of the experimental children on their friends and
neighbors. "If what we are finding is indeed diffusion, this is one
of the most optimistic findings possible," she said.

Shortly thereafter, evidence of another kind of diffusion turned
up: diffusion downward, toward the younger brothers and sisters
of children in the program, as a result of the weekly home visits.
This so fascinated Dr. Gray that she is now running a much
larger study, as director of the new Peabody Demonstration and
Research Center for Early Education, to find out how to make
the most of this phenomenon.

Her plan is to concentrate on mothers who have more than
one child under the age of four. Thus, anything the mothers
learn will benefit more than one preschool child. From a large
housing project, the center has selected three such groups of
mothers and children. The children in the first group are spending two years in a special preschool; their mothers have little
contact with the center. Those in the second group attend a similar preschool, but in addition their mothers must work in the
preschool one day a week, observing other children and new techniques. The third group does not go to school, but the center
sends a special teacher into the children's homes once a week.

By thus isolating the various ingredients of her earlier project,
Dr. Gray hopes to discover which ones have the greatest impact
on the family as a whole. While the progress of the children of
target age will be of interest to her, a more crucial comparison,
she says, will be that of their younger brothers and sisters. She
expects that the second group of mothers, target children, and
younger siblings will show the greatest change.

Human beings generally change most soon after exposure to

a new environment. The biggest changes in college students seem to occur during their freshman year; the rate of change slows down after the novelty of a situation wears off. For researchers who work with children, this can prove extremely discouraging—especially if they use control groups.

"People in industry have long known that any new thing can be done well for one year; that is the Hawthorne effect," says David P. Weikart, director of the Perry Preschool Project in Ypsilanti, Michigan. As he has found out since 1962, when his program began, this initial spurt of progress is difficult to maintain.

More than any other researcher, Weikart deliberately stacked the cards against himself by selecting the most disadvantaged children he could find, with IQ's so low as to fall in the category of mentally retarded. He had to do this because the project's funds came from the Department of Special Education, of which he is director. Thus, all the children involved were diagnosed as "educable mentally retarded, without organic involvement," on the theory that their handicap was the result of cultural deprivation, not physical injury. Their IQ's averaged about 79 (the lowest IQ generally considered within the normal range is 85). As Weikart puts it, it was the sort of project for which "if you get any applications, throw them away. Those who apply don't need it."

When he started his cognitively oriented curriculum for children as young as three, it seemed revolutionary. He offered them two years of training before they entered the regular kindergartens, with nursery school in the morning and a home visit one afternoon a week.

The teachers were introduced into homes with the statement, "This is a new program to help children do better in school"— a statement carefully calculated to avoid the image of a social worker who attempts to resolve marital problems or tell parents how to raise their children. Mothers were encouraged to be present and observe the lessons.

At least one-third of the mothers became thoroughly involved in the teaching process as a result of these two-hour visits, though their enthusiasm was sometimes misguided. One mother was so anxious to let nothing interfere with her youngest child's tutoring sessions that she just sat there with a strap in her hand, to keep the older children away, reported the teacher who visited her home. Others tended to compete with their children in working out the puzzles and games brought by the teacher. A few were natural teachers, like the one who modeled herself on the visitor, after observing her carefully for two months, and who now teaches just as effectively.

Another large group of mothers—perhaps 50 percent—were moderately involved, according to the teachers. They observed from time to time, but mostly they made casual comments, such as "That's good," or gave their children a hug. Even this reinforced the program somewhat and helped the child, although the mother did not learn to teach on her own.

A handful of others—a little more than 15 percent—simply retreated to another room and turned on the TV, relieved that a free baby sitter was giving them a few minutes' respite. In some cases, they were not even at home when the teacher came at her appointed time. Considering that these families were at the lowest end of the C.D. (Cultural Deprivation) index—a group so alienated that nobody else had seemed to reach them—the teachers felt much encouraged by the number of mothers who did participate in the teaching.

The woman with the strap in her hand may have had the wrong technique, but she had the right idea about the importance of a one-to-one relationship, judging from a study made by Weikart. When he examined the differences between the children whose IQ's had increased most during the program and those whose IQ's had increased least, he was surprised to find that the low-gainers were usually those whose brothers or sisters had tried to participate in the tutoring sessions. He concluded that this participation had two bad effects: It interfered with actual learning during the home visits, and it also produced "poor attenders" who would learn less in the small-group setting of the nursery school. Another factor that distinguished the low-gainers was their parents' extreme strictness. Apparently only those children whose parents were not too strict could benefit from the program.

In the nursery school itself, the method thought to be most effective at first was Verbal Bombardment—which meant that the teachers directed a steady stream of questions and comments at the children throughout the day. "It is this Bombardment that seems to produce dramatic growth in intelligence," Weikart wrote in 1964. Otherwise, the school's two-and-a-half hour curriculum looked pretty standard.

But the teachers themselves found Verbal Bombardment difficult. "You just kept talking almost all the time," recalled one, with horror. "All the teachers reacted. They didn't want to teach in this way. One of the kids came up to me and tried to close my mouth—I got the message! They seemed to tune us off like a TV set; they had learned this even before coming to school. And the teachers thought they were teaching vocabulary. Now they realize there are other things more important than just vocabularly. You need to know the child really has the *idea*, not just a name, a word for things. He must understand big, little, large, small."

At the end of the first year, the first group of four-year-olds in the program was given IQ tests and compared with a matched control group. From a starting average of 79 on the Stanford-Binet they had jumped to an IQ of 91, while the controls scored only 82. But after a year of regular kindergarten—which was the controls' first experience with school—the controls nearly caught up with the experimental group, which fell back slightly.

This second-year slump greatly discouraged the staff. After a year in the first grade, however, it was the control group's turn to slump, bringing them back close to 80, while the experimental children rallied and scored around 90.

The children who started at age three showed a similar pattern. Their IQ's rose from 79 to 91 after the first year of nursery school, then declined slightly, to 89, during the second year, while the controls remained consistently around 80. After both groups had attended kindergarten—the controls' first year of school—the controls went up to 83. However, the experimental group no longer declined. Recovering from the second-year slump, it remained at an IQ level of 91 or slightly higher, while the controls would probably suffer their slump during first grade.

Another wave of children entered the Perry preschool at age three the following year. These were the first three-year-olds to mix with a group of four-year-olds who had had one year of nursery school. From an average IQ of 81 when they entered, they jumped to an IQ of 101 after their first year—a gain of more than 20 points, and the biggest scored by any group in the program. But after their second year they, too, declined, to approximately 95. The difference between them and the controls was still highly significant—nearly 16 points of IQ—but it could be expected to dwindle after the controls started school.

Disappointed, Weikart decided to change the curriculum. The Verbal Bombardment would be focused on certain concepts, such as "some" or "all," he said. "It's not just language, but the ability to classify we are after. Until now, our teachers thought primarily in terms of enrichment. Now we are working toward the creation of foundations—foundations theoretically determined by Piaget to be essential."

The new, Piaget-based curriculum is still being worked out.

Besides classification and seriation (these are prereading and pre-math skills) and the kind of symbolization that leads to language, Weikart plans to emphasize dramatic play and impulse control. The latter, he explained, involves letting the child do his own planning. When he comes to school, he is given a choice of blocks, dolls, paints, and so forth, but then he must stick with his decision, even though it may be hard for him.

"My biggest worry," says Weikart, "is that people will find Head Start and preschool programs in general do *not* help the culturally deprived child; or else, if a few of them do help, that people will assume just any kindergarten program with a trained teacher will do the trick. The concept of unequal education for children who are unequal is not too well accepted." After his experience with these children, he changed his opinion about the age at which compensatory education should begin. He now believes the point seems to be two years of age or even earlier —not three.

The preschool of the future will be very different from what exists today, Weikart believes. There will be trained persons to go into homes and show mothers how to teach. They will bring technical equipment and games into the home. They will turn the homes into more educationally productive situations. They will work with *all* the young children in the home. One teacher could work with eight to ten families, reaching about twenty to forty youngsters. This is an economically feasible way of doing preschool education. Now the school costs $1,500 per year per child without the research. It would be only $300 a year for weekly home visits.

In certain cases, Weikart recognizes, day-care centers for very young children will prove necessary. But which is the *critical* variable? Maybe it's getting the mother to use alternative methods of dealing with her children—explain, reason with them—maybe it's something entirely different. The expense is so great, and the need so enormous, says Weikart, that we can afford only those things that are critical.

And what about middle-class children? If Weikart has his way, they'll continue going to ordinary nursery schools, like the one attended by his own child. "Oh, it's just delightful," he says about his daughter's happy experiences in nursery school, and the new words she comes home with every day.

America's disadvantaged children—a group of staggering but perhaps still manageable size—make up roughly one-third of the total child population.

In Israel, on the other hand, such children make up the majority. The rapid influx of illiterate Oriental Jews from Yemen, Morocco, and Iraq a decade ago completely changed the population of the Israeli schools, bringing the number of culturally disadvantaged children to more than *two-thirds* of those in the nation's elementary classes. This led to soaring rates of school failure, beginning in first grade. By 1957 it had become clear that such academic failures also produced marked deterioration in the children's social and emotional adjustment. Long before the American wave of interest in the preschool years, Israeli educators then pointed the finger of blame at the kindergarten.

Unlike the United States, Israel requires all five-year-olds to attend kindergarten. Originally their kindergarten teachers, like ours, relied heavily on free-play periods, during which the children could use blocks, paints, or other materials as they pleased; this was supposed to be enrichment, and the general idea was not to interfere too much with the process, which seemed to work well with intellectually active middle-class children.

As the epidemic of school failures raged on, however, a study by Dr. Sarah Smilansky of the Henrietta Szold Institute in Jerusalem concluded that the nondirective, "progressive" methods employed had failed with these children.

A deliberate program of guided intellectual development was then worked out for an experimental group of Oriental kindergarteners. Their teachers were urged to see themselves as part of the total school system, and actively to prepare the children for first grade. Under close supervision from the experimenters, the teachers broke up their classes into small groups and worked either with these groups or with individual children. New tests were developed to help the teachers become aware of each child's level of achievement in each sphere—cognitive development, verbal ability, general information, concentration.

"We emphasized that each child is potentially able to overcome his deficiencies," wrote Dr. Smilansky, "that a child's failure to respond lies not in his basic ineptitude, but in his inability to catch on to the 'game' of communication with the teacher." Breaking through to each child's world would require specific knowledge of his particular competencies and deficiencies. Therefore the teachers were trained to use the detailed test findings on each child as a starting point, and teach him exactly what he lacked. Later on they would retest, formally and informally, to discover what, in fact, each child was learning. In this way they would no longer be without an anchor for their work.

The classes were enormous by American standards: thirty to forty children, the normal size in Israel. All the children were five years old, all came from slum districts, and all their parents had emigrated from Yemen, Morocco, or Iraq at about the same time. The teachers were those already present in the schools that had been selected for the experiment, but they received additional training from the Smilansky group.

By the end of one year, the IQ's of the experimental children had gone up an average of 19 points on the Stanford-Binet; those of the controls, who attended traditional kindergartens, had gone up only 12 points. Both in this respect and in their improved verbal ability, the Oriental children in the Smilansky kinder-

gartens were brought up to par with lower-class European children who, it was known, generally did well in first and second
grades. The final test—their actual progress through elementary
school—was yet to come.

Despite this apparently successful experiment, Israeli educators
decided that the cultural gap between the Oriental and the European children was far too obvious by the age of three to ignore
until kindergarten. A whole spectrum of free nursery schools
was then set up for more than 20,000 children from culturally
disadvantaged homes. Some were Montessori schools. Others
taught reading and writing at the age of four. In addition, a system of home visitors was tried out: Volunteer social workers
went into the homes of new or expectant parents, taught them
how to play with young children, and left behind a set of toys
which the government "lent" them for a year. According to Professor Benjamin Bloom, Israel is years ahead of the United States
in solving this problem.

From Bereiter to Smilansky, through revolution or evolution,
all the preschool programs that have had some success in providing disadvantaged children with the skills they will need in
school evidently share these traits:

They deliberately plan sequences that will lead the children
to specific educational goals.

They realize that time is their most precious commodity, and
that each activity must be selected for its maximum contribution
to learning.

Last but not least, their teachers work with small groups or
individual children—hardly ever with the class as a whole.

Chapter 8

DAY CARE: THE PROBLEM
NOBODY WANTS TO FACE

"I KNOW a lot of people say that mothers shouldn't work," Vice President Humphrey declared recently, "but I have been brought up to believe that what is, is." He called the lack of adequate day-care facilities for children of working mothers one of the greatest problems of tomorrow's America.

Though nobody wants to face it, this lack is also the single most urgent problem of preschool children today. One out of every four mothers of children under the age of six is in the labor force. The number of such mothers has doubled since 1950. Four million American preschoolers now have mothers who work. Yet only 225,000 children of all ages can be squeezed into the nation's licensed day-care facilities.

What happens to the others? According to Katherine Oettinger, chief of the U.S. Children's Bureau, 38,000 children under six have no care at all while their mothers work. Presumably they are just locked up in their homes. Twice as many infants and toddlers are looked after by a youngster under the age of sixteen.

Another 600,000 preschoolers spend the day in what is euphemistically called "family day care." In theory this sounds fine: The mother leaves her child with a friendly neighbor, who takes in several other children at the same time, for a small fee. In New York City, where public day-care programs have waiting lists as long as their actual enrollment, and where the more centers are opened the longer the waiting lists become, a study has just been made to find out what family day care is really like. Since the Board of Health actually licensed only twenty-five homes for family day care in the entire city, this study looked into the unlicensed homes which take in some 25,000 New York children, more than half of them under the age of six.

One of the interviewers for the Medical and Health Research Association of New York City, which did this study, still has nightmares about some of the places she visited. She recalls a day-care "mother" in Central Harlem who took as many as four children at a time into her cluttered apartment, getting $15 a week for each child. The hall was used by drug addicts and "winos." In the apartment itself "you had to fight your way past torn mattresses, broken springs, all kinds of stuff which she collected—but there was not a single toy in sight," says Anna Graziano, who spent months doing this research. A four-month-old baby lay in a dark, dank bedroom on a big double bed without any barriers to prevent him from falling. "While I was there, his bottle fell to the floor several times," Miss Graziano reports, "and the woman just picked it up and gave it back to him without washing it or making a single comment. Otherwise, she paid no attention to him. There was another little boy of about eighteen months who kept making noises, so she told me to wait a minute, took him to another room, and came back saying, 'Now we can chat.' But he howled so much that after half an hour I insisted on going in to look at him, though she didn't want me to. I opened the door and saw this child shrieking—she had tied him to his crib with diapers around both his hands and feet."

The woman knew nothing about the background of the children in her charge, points out Miss Graziano. She knew neither their age nor even their correct last names. "I asked if she had the mothers' addresses or telephone numbers so she could reach them during the day in case of emergency, but she said, 'Oh, no, I forgot to get it.' As to taking the children outdoors, her reply was, 'I took this youngster out to the street once, but it was too much bother.'"

Some of the women who take in children are drunkards. Many more, according to Miss Graziano, are physically ill—and their illness is the very reason for their doing this kind of work. She recalls a harassed twenty-year-old girl who had previously worked as a salesgirl but had lost her job because of a severe anemia which left her always tired. The girl lived in a three-bedroom house with her parents, her own out-of-wedlock daughter (aged two), her uncle, her aunt, and their two children. In this home she also took three other children for day care, being paid $32 a week for all three. She hated what she was doing. She had lost control over the six children to the extent that she did not even bother to find out what part of the house they were in. One youngster, aged four, did nothing but cry all day long, sitting alone on the top step of the porch. The girl said he was "spoiled."

The children's routine in most family day-care homes is limited to breakfast, TV cartoons, lunch, nap, and TV. The study showed that 34 percent of the homes lacked play materials of any kind. In 25 percent of the homes the children were never taken out-of-doors. As many as 84 percent of the homes were rated inadequate because they violated the Health Code, or because the children were severely neglected.

There were a few glowing exceptions, such as the day-care "mother" in Central Harlem who ran what amounted to a first-rate nursery school in her house despite incredible difficulties.

She had three children of her own under the age of six. To supplement her husband's meager income, she took care of four more, going about it in a highly professional way. She had cleared her living room of nearly everything except a long table along one wall, where some children were busy with crayons. "I need the space for the children to run about," she explained. Her walls were covered with paintings—her own and those of the children. There were blackboards, easels, and a variety of educational toys freely available. She had printed instructions for the children's mothers. At various times of day she managed to drop some children off at school and pick up others, taking the whole brood along with her on each trip. Despite these interruptions, she preserved large blocks of time for the children to play with clay, paints, or whatever she had scheduled for the day. She was also keenly aware of each child's difficulties and feelings.

On Miss Graziano's treks in and out of many slums in some of the city's most dangerous neighborhoods, she was sometimes struck by such extraordinary victories of the human spirit. But for the most part, the children were given no more than the bare necessities for physical survival.

Throughout their study, the interviewers were assailed by desperate women who begged them to help find good day-care services for their children. They would try any trick to attract the interviewers' attention, hoping it might somehow lead them to space in a day-care center. The study's associate director, Milton Willner, a social worker with long experience in day care, concluded that two kinds of programs were urgently needed: a training program for women who would run licensed family day care for up to five children in their homes, bolstered by periodic inspections to make sure they provided enough play materials, nap facilities, and fresh air; and many, many more day-care centers, including some for children under the age of three.

Before such programs can be expanded, or even begun, the

attitude of the public must change, Willner believes. It is not only a matter of money, although the cost of good day care runs high. It is the reluctance to interfere in what is generally regarded as a family responsibility, the desire to prevent mothers from working, and "a sense of guilt which weighs heavily on the field of day care when it is confronted with a request to accept a child."

Even when the child is between the ages of three and six—the standard age for full day care—and even when space exists, the social workers who rule these centers must first establish that there is a social need—that it isn't just a case of the mother wanting to get rid of her children and go to work, as one welfare worker put it.

"Suppose you have to go to work for financial reasons," says Willner, "and you want to find a good day-care center for your four-year-old. You go to one of the family agencies that run such centers and ask them for help. First they'll do a study. If they find you're a healthy kind of person, you get along with your husband and your children, and you simply want to work, you're sure to be turned down flat. But if you have marital difficulties and problems with your children—ah! then they'll lick their lips, take your child, and give you counseling."

This typifies the arrogance of many social workers in this field, who believe that no woman is fit to make decisions about her own life without their help. Their attitude tends to squelch efforts at providing decent facilities on a large scale, or making sure that every young child has access to certain services and care.

Those who have seen the actual conditions into which thousands of American preschoolers are being pushed by the lack of day care cannot be blamed if they feel that nobody listens to them. During World War II, when it became not only acceptable but positively patriotic for mothers to work, enough nurseries and day-care centers suddenly blossomed, with government aid, to accommodate about 1,600,000 children. Today, when the number of working women exceeds the wartime total by 6 million, day-care centers have shrunk to one-sixth their wartime capacity.

While the nation gave Head Start $150 million for its first summer program, it appropriated only $7 million for day care—and that went mostly for better licensing procedures. The licensing that existed until then generally applied only to such things as toilet and fire regulations; few states had any requirements concerning the day-care center staffs. Better licensing was indeed essential; but it would not relieve the desperate need for services.

The most desperate mothers of all are those with children under the age of three. A startling total of 1,600,000 American youngsters under the age of three have mothers who work. When these women look for day care, "they come up against a stern wall of disapproval behind which is a vacuum of services," declares Mrs. Oettinger. "We did try to hold back the ocean. We always said the only place for the child under three was at home. Yet at this very minute children as young as two to four weeks are in inadequate arrangements made of necessity. We don't condone it, but babies are suffering—and we should see that they are in appropriate settings."

To find out what an appropriate setting would be like for such young babies, the Children's Bureau is now supporting several experimental programs, including one run by Head Start's Dr. Julius Richmond and Dr. Bettye Caldwell, who had written the ill-fated *Head Start Daily Activities* booklet number two.

This extraordinary Children's Center, in Syracuse, New York, violates every convention about day care as normally practiced in the United States: It takes babies as young as six months of age (all its clientele is under three), and it deliberately stimulates their intellectual development. "At the beginning," recalls Dr. Caldwell, "I almost had to apologize for setting up this program." Several of the experts whom she called on to help plan the center rebuked her for even attempting it.

As Dr. Richmond explains it, "There's a tremendous bias against day care in the field of child welfare, due to overinterpretation of data. Since group care under certain circumstances is bad, people assume all group care is bad. But after having seen the real circumstances, we felt no great qualms of conscience. We felt it was ethically appropriate for us to provide better care than what these children were receiving."

The "real" circumstances he mentions came to light when he and Dr. Caldwell did a study of one hundred babies from very-low-income families whose mothers brought them to the Upstate Medical Center in Syracuse for check-ups. This showed something that many people suspected all along, but that his study documented. "About one-third of the babies were *not* cared for by their mothers during their first year of life," he says. "Now this would not have come out if we had not gone into the homes and studied the families; since the mothers brought the babies into the clinic, one would normally assume that they cared for their babies themselves.

"Actually, the babies had multiple mothers; they were parked with baby sitters or others, often under circumstances that would make our hair stand on end."

The Children's Center opened in 1964 as a five-year demonstration of how "culturally determined mental retardation" could be prevented among high-risk infants and toddlers. The idea was to promote *both* emotional-social development and cognitive growth with equal vigor. These are symbiotic—one does not develop at the expense of the other, emphasizes Dr. Caldwell, a psychologist who is the mother of twins. It is important to develop these children's sense of trust in adults and in events, she believes. The center arranges situations that lead the children to certain cognitive operations—classification, conceptualization, learning sets. At all times, it tries to provide an atmosphere in which infants and children can thrive, not merely grow.

Physically, the center consists of a narrow old building formerly used by medical students, and a large, reconverted trailer specifically adapted for the babies. It stands next to a spacious yard with swings, sandpiles, and climbing equipment. Behind each classroom there is a closetlike area in which researchers can observe the children through a one-way mirror without disturbing them.

As I walked up to the second floor, I met a half-dozen toddlers, about eighteen months to two years old, on their way out with their teacher. They were going to a farm to see the animals and, hopefully, ride some ponies while held by a teen-ager. "We've already taken the older group out. They had a wonderful time," said Dr. Caldwell.

From a researchers' nook I watched the two- to three-year-olds having juice and cookies as a story was read to them. There were two teachers for eight tots—a ratio of one teacher for four children, which Dr. Caldwell calls an absolute minimum. This ratio was often improved by the addition of student teachers. Each child, I was told, had one staff person primarily responsible for him, who cared for him when he awoke from his nap. Each one received the concentrated, individual attention of a teacher once in the morning and once in the afternoon, for at least half an hour at a time.

Although the center supposedly provides group care, to which many experts object for this age group, in practice it offers a highly individualized type of care. Its unhurried atmosphere hides the fact that the currriculum is carefully programmed to try and match each child's particular level of intellectual development.

Even the babies under one year of age do finger painting on

plastic trays and take part in special learning games. They may listen to various sounds—bells, whispering, and stones in a box—or smell many odors, including vinegar. A one-year-old may learn object permanence: The teacher puts a toy behind a barrier to see whether the baby can find it; later on, she may use two detours, placing two different covers over the same toy. A slightly older child may work on the toy-string problem: He learns to pull a string to reach a toy, a lesson in cause and effect. Once a month they are given very informal tests to see whether they have grasped certain concepts, such as "bigger" or "smaller."

The trailer in which all this takes place was originally used by the crew of a construction company. Airy and neat, it holds seven cribs for the babies to nap in, a large bathroom, a large indoor play area, and a kitchen area. It cost $3,400, plus another $1,000 for installation. Since the children's mothers have varied schedules, the bulk of planned activities takes place between 9 A.M. and 4 P.M.

While I was there the babies returned from their outdoor play in the yard, all aglow. Some had runny noses, which a teacher wiped. Most of the children were Negro. An attractive Danish teacher changed the smallest baby's diaper. Seated on a high chair, a seventeen-month-old was about to start his concept learning session.

"Do you want to play a game?" asked his teacher, a pleasant, matronly woman who frequently cuddled her charges. She placed two metal cups before the boy—one small and shallow, the other big and deep. Then she hid a Fruit Loop (a small, colored cereal loop) under the small cup. "Let's look under the little one," she said. Perhaps accidentally, the baby picked up the right cup, while the teacher exclaimed, "Good boy!" and clapped. The baby ate the cereal. On other trials, he occasionally chucked everything to the floor.

Dr. Caldwell considers the babies' training the most important step in the center's program. She had expected it to be the most difficult to arrange, but it turned out to be the easiest. She ran into real problems only when she tried to systematize the older children's program, probably for cultural reasons: While our culture takes it for granted that babies must be treated individually, any situation that looks like a nursery school makes teachers want to teach the whole group. She tried to get around this by setting up a platoon system, under which the children were split up into small subgroups. She also insisted that each child be read to or played with individually for at least an hour a day. This met with great resistance from the teachers at first, she reports. Working with such small groups is accepted in theory, but it just was not happening. The complaint was, "I won't ever have time to read to them again"—meaning as a group—or, "They all enjoy pasting!" Some teachers objected because they wanted nothing but free play. For others, structuring activities meant a rigid schedule. "The word 'structure' has nothing to do with discipline or schedule—it means basically *planning*," says Dr. Caldwell. "You *stage* things a bit. You give form and shape to them. A well-placed question is a good example of structure." Now, she says, they have arrived at a more comfortable balance between free and planned activities, though the group still exerts a tremendous pull and the older children's activities are still not as individualized as she would like.

To fit the schedules of working mothers, the center is open from 7:30 A.M. to 6 P.M. five days a week. All the children spend nights and weekends at home. The first twenty-three children who entered the center did so for a variety of reasons. One came because his mother had had a nervous breakdown and was sent to a mental hospital. Another, the youngest of four children in a stable and apparently happy family, where both parents worked, came because his mother wanted to prevent the difficulties his older brothers and sister had had in school. At his age—two and a half—they had all seemed bright and talked well, she said, but later they failed in school; she didn't want it to happen again.

The father of three other youngsters—aged three, two, and ten months—had died just before the baby's birth, leaving a total of ten children and a greatly overburdened mother. Some of the older children had already dropped out of school. Rather than break up the family by sending the children to separate foster homes—the mother simply could not cope with the situation any more—the Welfare Department decided to try the center, and it worked. Even though the mother required an operation and had to be hospitalized for a while, she managed to keep the family together, since the three youngest ones were taken care of during the day.

"Not all the children's mothers are working," points out Dr. Richmond. "Some are teen-agers who can't function as mothers because they haven't yet fulfilled their own narcissistic needs. One thing we learned very quickly: to have continuity in the child population, you've got to have transportation for the child. Parents will generally get their child to a car, even if they wouldn't bring the child by themselves. This means fighting the bias of middle-class people who often say, 'If they don't have the motivation, to hell with them!' We've done too much writing off of people of this kind—those who need it the most."

Because the center's program is so revolutionary, the first thing that had to be established was that it would do the children no harm. So far, the children seem to develop well on all counts: They have formed attachments to the staff, they get along well with each other, and their IQ's have shown a tendency to rise as they grow older, rather than decline with time, as happens with most high-risk babies.

By now this is no longer a test of group care for very young infants, states Bettye Caldwell. Rather, it is a test of whether any other kind of care can provide the necessary supplements for the child. These supplements cost nearly $200,000 per year, including research, for twenty-five children. The program could be run, without the research, for about $3,000 per year per child. The only alternative to the center is foster day care through the Department of Welfare, but finding foster homes for all the children who need help is just not realistic.

Day care *must* be expensive, if only because its first require-ment is a high ratio of teachers to children. In Israel, where the communal settlements called kibbutzim have a long history of group care for infants and toddlers, great sacrifices have been made to provide this ratio—usually one *metapelet*, or nurse, for every four children under the age of two—despite war and short-ages of all kinds.

If people really care, a variety of child-rearing patterns are possible without producing pathology, declares Dr. Leon Eisen-berg, professor of child psychiatry at Johns Hopkins, who has visited several kibbutzim. Though the mother is absent most of the day, she remains the central psychological figure to her child. This is multiple mothering, not deprivation. Describing the warmth of the metapelet and the general atmosphere of love and concern for all the children in the kibbutz, Dr. Eisenberg remarked that "if the children suffer from anything there, it's mother-poisoning, not mother-deprivation! There are mothers all over the place—and all making chicken-noodle soup!" Such an atmosphere leads children to expect good from all adults, he continued. But he warned that it doesn't usually happen in other types of institutions.

By cutting corners, reducing personnel, or packing in too many children, any institution can easily be turned into a snake pit. At best, an institution is a very unstable organism. It becomes particularly dangerous when dealing with human beings at their most vulnerable age.

Despite this danger, however, something must be done for

children in this age group, and it is easier to provide proper safe-
guards in day-care centers than in "black-market" family day
care. According to Dr. Caldwell, the climate of opinion on this
subject is changing rapidly. Suddenly a large number of organizations want to start their own centers for very young children.

This change in climate is partly due to the work of a small
but influential organization called Early Child Care Reexamined
(ECCR), which became interested in the problem a few years
ago. Its first conference was sparked by Dr. Caroline Chandler,
chief of the National Institute of Mental Health's center for
studies of mental health of children and youth, after a ques-
tionnaire she had sent out to every state in the Union revealed
"the incredible, woefully inadequate services almost everywhere."
The psychiatrists, pediatricians, and child-welfare experts who
attended this first conference decided to take a fresh look at the
whole infant field and clear up many common misconceptions—
particularly the notion that group care for children under three
was always bad. Although they clashed on many points, they
agreed that in certain cases group care was not only desirable,
but essential if one wished to avoid damage to the child's personality or cognition.

"I don't care under what label you start developing relationships with children," replied one ECCR psychiatrist when I
asked him what he thought of Dr. Caldwell's center. "In order
to work with cognitive development, you have to get involved
with the children—and only good can come of that! That is, if
you have warm people who don't treat babies like experimental
animals, but like human beings."

The department of psychiatry of Washington's Children's
Hospital, a cosponsor of the ECCR conferences, is planning to
open a day-care center of its own for high-risk babies, taking
them as soon after birth as possible. It will also try to develop
a new career for American women: trained nursery mothers who

can work in day-care centers. The training program, which will last about one year, will be modeled after that of the famed Metera Babies' Center in Athens, Greece.

All over the world, people who deal with the formative years of the most important possession a country has—its children— are important professionals, points out Dr. Allen Marans, director of this training project. "The kibbutz metapelet has prestige and professional security," he says. "The Soviet Union gives its day-care people high prestige. In France, the director of the crèche is a very important person in the community."

The staffs of American day-care centers, on the other hand, clearly lack both status and decent salaries. Although the number of centers has not grown much recently, their personnel shortages are worse than ever since fashionable new programs such as Head Start can offer much more in the way of money and pleasant working conditions. The day-care centers are particularly short of teachers. Education, in fact, has never been their forte. If there are qualified teachers, it's a nursery school; if it's custodial, it's day care, is the working definition of the difference between the two.

The problem greatly surpasses anything that has been attempted so far to solve it. Nor can it be solved, says Mrs. Oettinger, until the nation assumes the responsibility and obligation to see that children are given good care during their developmental stage. People are still ambivalent about this, she notes. She looks forward to the day when legislators and taxpayers agree that we must do it—like making sure that every child in the country is vaccinated against polio.

Dr. Marans puts it more bluntly: "The United States is really not a child-centered culture," he declares. "People are startled when I say that, but it's true."

Chapter 9

THE DISCOVERY OF
INFANCY

THE one-month-old baby—a healthy, normal little creature—lay in his crib, hooked up to electronic equipment that recorded his heartbeats. A bright red ball (held by an unseen researcher) entered the infant's field of vision, then disappeared behind a screen (where it was exchanged for a black cube), and, as if by magic, a black cube appeared at the other end.

"Bang went the baby's heartbeat—at one month of age!" reports Harvard University's Jerome S. Bruner, who observed this experiment at the Center for Cognitive Studies. When the heartbeat drops, this is a measure of attention; it shows the baby is attending to something.

Bruner, who "only recently dared work with children as young as three," has now joined the growing group of researchers who are discovering infancy as the most exciting and fruitful period of human life to study. Only a few years ago, the theory was that newborn babies couldn't see more than the difference between light and dark; that during their first three months of life they were so absorbed by their insides they could hardly react to the outside world; and that therefore their physical environment mattered little, so long as the baby's mother provided food and comfort. Scientists of various breeds have just begun to realize, however, that infants register far more of their environment than any but the most doting mothers have given them credit for—and not only in terms of the emotions involved.

"Children are able to discriminate more things in the first months of life than we ever dreamed of," says Bruner. They can distinguish half tones of color, diagonals. On the day of birth, they can track a triangle with their eyes. By the time they are one month old, they can spot the identity of objects, and know when something has been changed.

In other experiments, polygraphs have been taped to newborn babies' heads to record the change in electrical potential every time the eyelids move. Blinking lights have flashed before young babies as cameras whirred overhead, recording every tiny, uncoordinated gesture. Blips on a piece of paper have recorded every time the child sucked on a nipple. Tape recorders have registered each babyish cry or gurgle. Much of this material was then fed into computers, to be sorted out and analyzed.

"Today we are launched on what amounts to a national renaissance in child research," declares Dr. Stanley F. Yolles, director of the National Institute of Mental Health. Most of the scientists interested in human behavior have become swept up in some aspect of it. As a result, a new brand of child psychology is unfolding. Not long ago, 93 percent of all child development studies were done without any direct observations of the child himself, he points out. Now, instead of curbstone opinions, the researchers collect mountains of facts at the scene of the action.

Much of the recent work on infancy has centered on the first five days of life, when infants are usually in a hospital anyway and so easily available for research. "Older" infants—from three to nine months of age—have proved much more difficult to come by. When he needed such children for his work on perception, Yale University psychologist Dr. William Kessen advertised in local newspapers, begging mothers to bring their infants for ten or fifteen minutes of observation. He paid the volunteers nothing but taxi fare. Unfortunately, few mothers volunteered more than once.

"We are shamefully ignorant about what happens between the time the baby leaves the hospital and the time he shows up in nursery school," comments Dr. Kessen. "Yet this is exactly when all things of importance take place. We still depend almost exclusively on Piaget's observations of his own three children for this period."

One reason for this ignorance is the obsession many psychologists have shown, until recently, for such topics as the comparative merits of breast-feeding and bottle-feeding, the perils of early toilet training, or the much more serious matter of maternal deprivation.

Shortly after World War II, the concern about maternal deprivation reached its peak. Dr. René Spitz's poignant movies of babies in an institution showed how infants who were deprived of their mothers or of adequate substitutes increasingly lost interest in their surroundings, stopped playing, stopped hoping, and even stopped crying. The institution was a foundling home, in which the babies had been placed because their mothers did not have the money to support them. After their mothers stopped nursing them at three months of age, the babies received almost no attention or stimulation. The busy nurses fed them according to a fixed schedule, diapered them regularly, but had no time to do more. Spitz compared these babies' progressive deterioration, which he called "hospitalism," with the healthy development of another group of infants in a nursery attached to a women's prison. The first group of mothers was presumably normal, though poor; the second group consisted of mentally retarded women, delinquent minors, and psychopaths. Yet the babies in the second group thrived since their mothers were allowed to care for them every day during their first year. Their developmental quotients rose from 97 at the age of two or three months to an average of 112 at the age of four or five months, settling back to 100—the norm for their age—just before their first birthdays. During the same period, the babies in the foundling home sank from an average development quotient of 131 at the age of two or three months to a mere 72 at ten to twelve months, as Dr. Spitz's movies showed in pathetic detail. Most people who saw these movies left with the firm conviction that infants need full-time love and care from their mothers, or else they will perish.

Though babies normally learn to sit without support by the age of ten months, infants in an orphanage in Teheran (Iran) became so apathetic and retarded that fewer than half of them learned to sit up alone by the age of two years, Professor Wayne Dennis, of Brooklyn College, reported in 1960. At the age of four, 85 percent of them still failed to walk alone. Even the sequence of motor skills which they developed took a peculiar turn, despite the general belief that such sequences are fixed by built-in mechanisms. Instead of creeping before standing up and walking, these children scooted on their rear ends—propelling themselves forward from a sitting position, with their hands, along the slippery floor. Children who could not yet stand up by themselves by the age of two or three knew how to get around quite efficiently in this fashion.

Similar evidence piled up from other parts of the world. An influential survey by Dr. John Bowlby, of Great Britain, brought all institutional care of infants into disrepute. Various studies showed that the earlier in life maternal deprivation started, and the longer it lasted, the worse were its results. If a baby were institutionalized for only a few months and given excellent care thereafter, the bad effects might be largely corrected. But if deprivation started in infancy and lasted for as long as three years, the damage could never be undone.

To avoid trauma, it appeared, babies needed to be with their mothers twenty-four hours a day; thus, day-care centers were evil. Part-time care by anybody other than the mother was evil. Any separation from her at any time carried serious dangers; even mothers who sent their youngsters to nursery school for a couple of hours a day were often accused of wanting to "dump" them there. In reaction, nursery schools concentrated on creating a homelike atmosphere in the classroom, with the teacher taking over the mother's role, and researchers spent their efforts on studies of how the children reacted to their brief separation from the mother.

As the new cognitive psychologists see the situation, however, the most dangerous element in the orphanages was not the children's separation from their mothers, but the fact that nobody provided them with any sort of stimulation. Babies in such institutions spent their whole time waiting for something interesting to happen to them—and eventually gave up. To protect them from drafts and from getting their heads stuck between bars, their cribs were lined with white covers, which acted like blinders; they could see nothing on either side of them. The ceilings were also white, without anything interesting to look at. Nobody talked to them, and they heard precious little speech of any kind. They had no toys. They took their nourishment alone, from bottles that were propped up for them.

Besides having nothing interesting done to them, these infants never had the opportunity to do anything that might produce interesting results—no incentive for the kind of repeated, intentional efforts that lead babies to learn new skills. J. McV. Hunt believes that these two lacks may have more to do with the infants' drop in developmental quotient than any lack of a strongly emotional, personal relationship with the mother, at least during the first year of life.

Psychologists throughout the country are now trying various experiments to see what kind of enrichment can best accelerate infants' intellectual development. Hunt himself is working with brightly colored tassels, miniature umbrellas, and odd-shaped boxes, to be hung onto ordinary or specially designed "wiggly" cribs. The cribs-plus-mobiles then go into Illinois private homes for the pleasure of four-week-old infants, who can make the mobiles move by "wiggling" their cribs. The babies who have these tassels learn to blink—a landmark in development—about three weeks earlier than do other babies from similar homes. They also show a definite preference for the familiar mobiles at two months of age, followed a month later by an interest in the unfamiliar ones.

Any experiment carried on in a private home is difficult to control, however. Therefore Hunt and his collaborator, Dr. Ina Uzgiris, have started a similar study in an orphanage in Teheran. They want to give these infants a chance to produce truly dramatic effects on their environment. Once again they are using tassels, but here they have added a tape recorder. So now a two-months-old baby in this experiment needs only to shake his legs and—presto!—the tassel begins to dance (it is attached to one of his legs by a string), and music begins to play.

In Massachusetts, Dr. Burton L. White, of Harvard University, has spent the past eight years studying normal infants in a nursery connected with a state hospital—the nearest thing he could find to an old-fashioned orphanage. Here, too, infants spent their first four months lying in white-lined cribs that cut off the world outside. White became interested in the development of what he called "visually directed reaching" in these infants. As early as two months of age, when the infants first discovered their hands, they began to swipe at objects—a closed-fist move-ment which naturally did not result in grasping anything. Next came a Piaget-type reach: The baby raised one hand toward the object, looked back and forth from hand to object, and eventu-ally made contact with it. Finally the baby learned to reach, and grasp, objects that were held up above him.

The institutionalized babies took three months to progress from the swipe to the top-level reach. Was this delay inevitable? White wondered. Or could it be reduced by enriching the babies' environment? He had already observed a sudden increase in the babies' attention to their surroundings when they were transferred to large, open-sided cribs at around four months of age.

For his experiment, White selected nineteen infants who were only six days old. He started them out with one month of extra handling by a nurse, who would provide physical stimulation twenty minutes a day. At the age of one month and one week the infants were taken out of their bland, featureless white world and placed in a riot of colors: There were multicolored printed sheets with animal designs, flowered bumpers, and a large stabile, somewhat like a barbell, which featured a shiny ball at either end. At the same time, the babies' mattresses were flattened, to allow more freedom of motion than the soft, sagging mattresses on which they usually lay on their backs. Three times a day, after their feedings, the babies were placed on their tummies for fifteen minutes. While they were in this position, the front crib bumpers were replaced by clear plastic, offering them a view of all the ward activities. Almost at once the infants began to rear up their heads like elephants, to see what was going on.

This brave new world seemed almost too rich for the youngest infants at first, White reports. He feels he did not quite succeed in matching their level of development, since some of the younger ones cried a bit more than usual and paid less attention to their surroundings. However, once they reached the age of two and a half months, they really took to it—they seemed exhilarated, he says. They spent hours staring up at the stabiles, pawing them, trying to feel them. Apparently they were terribly pleased by the whole business: They smiled at objects, vocalized, chuckled away in a manner no other institutionalized child in the hospital did.

To provide a better match, White slowed down on the enrichment in his next experiment. After the month of extra handling, he gave the new group of infants a transitional period with only one bit of novelty: two pacifiers, attached on either side of the crib, in the center of two bright red-and-white targets, designed to draw the infants' attention. The babies graduated to the fully enriched surroundings at two months and one week of age, and were then treated in the same fashion as the first group until the age of four months.

The results of these experiments surpassed anything White had expected. Both groups of infants learned to reach for objects above them in about *half the time* it took those who had remained in the bland environment. The first group reduced the learning time by about six and a half weeks. The second group did even better, cutting it down by nearly eight weeks.

"I think we've shown clearly that enrichment procedures can produce remarkable effects on the course of early development," declares White, who is obviously excited about his findings. Once a child operates at a higher level, he is bringing in more information, which should make his cognitive development proceed more swiftly.

"For thousands of years, until now, the formal efforts of educators have been concentrated on children between the ages of six and sixteen," he says. "Implicit in this is the effort to teach children to think the way we do—to teach language, logic, math, and pump adult skills into immature brains. Adults have learned from experience that children don't respond to this much before six, except when the teacher is awfully clever, like O. K. Moore or Bruner." But now, thanks to Jean Piaget, White foresees a new science of education which will study the youngest children's own ways of learning, as opposed to the ways of adults. Piaget showed, says White, that in the everyday experiences of the child lie the origins of curiosity; that there are exciting possibilities; that these things can be moved around, for the child does respond to effort; that there is order in what the child does.

White believes his own work may have the most effect on the infants' motivation. By the time he is through enriching their lives, at five months, "they are very good babies—in every way. They are the kids who milk the most out of the available situation," he says. He would like to be able to continue working with them, matching their development every step of the way, but in view of the general ignorance about infants he believes he cannot afford to do so. Instead, he will continue to study how certain responses of infants can be accelerated by changing their environment. "I feel I've got my hands full for the next fifteen years with the first five months of life," he says.

Similar studies are now going on in Russia—in fact, much of the research on infants that American scientists are now pursuing was pioneered by Russians. Moscow University psychologists are studying the development of grasping movements in infants from birth to six months, as well as sucking movements, defense reactions (such as the eye blink) and the orienting reflex—the eye or head movements by which a child shows that he can predict certain events. A Leningrad psychologist has investigated orienting responses to sound in babies as young as two hours of age.

Soviet scientists have made particular headway in studying the orienting reflex and other evidence of attention. However, American scientists often use more sophisticated equipment. For example, the technique of recording an infant's heartbeats as a measure of attention is an American invention. Until it was developed, there was no way of knowing whether an infant was actually looking at something, or just staring blankly. With the help of this technique, Dr. Jerome Kagan, of Harvard's Department of Social Relations, has been able to show that the attention of infants is at its peak when they see something just a little unfamiliar—neither too novel nor too repetitious. This fits in very neatly with Hunt's theory about the problem of the match, and the need to find just the right degree of incongruity for each child.

Full of vigor and very informal, Dr. Kagan explains his work: On the fourteenth floor of the William James Hall he runs a lab with elaborate equipment where 130 infants are brought to be tested at four, eight, and thirteen months of age, then again at ages two, three, and four. It is one of the biggest longitudinal studies in the country. The children are all first-borns and white and come from intact families. Though none of the parents is on welfare, they range from some who did not finish elementary school to others who have Ph.D.'s; about one-third of them are workers.

The four-months-old babies in Dr. Kagan's lab were shown three kinds of faces: one the mere outline of a face; one flesh-colored sculpture of a regular male face; and a distorted version of the same face, in which the eyes, nose, and mouth were rearranged. Unanimously, they gave most attention to the well-defined, regular face; in fact, they reacted with a cardiac deceleration of about eight to ten beats, whereas the other faces barely affected the rate of their heartbeats. They also smiled at the regular face three times more frequently than at the distorted version.

When this test was repeated with eight-months-old babies, however, few of the regular faces drew much attention; the largest cardiac decelerations were registered for the distorted version. The reason for this, according to Kagan, lies in the babies' progress in classifying their environment. At four months, it took the infants a few seconds to smile at the regular face, as if they had first to study it carefully, for their schema of a face was not yet fully established. A schema, Dr. Kagan explained, is a representation of an external pattern, much as an artist's illustration is a representation of an event. By eight months, the schema of a face was so well assimilated by the infants that an ordinary human face held little challenge for them.

There is pleasure in the act of matching unfamiliar things to a schema, Kagan believes. He agrees with Piaget that the infant smiles not only for social reasons, but also because he is happy to have recognized something. At such times, says Kagan, the infant has "an 'aha' reaction. Large cardiac decelerations and smiles are most likely to occur to stimuli that seem to elicit tiny, quiet cognitive discoveries—miniature versions of Archimedes' 'Eureka!' "

Kagan's lab has devised a variety of new tests that measure how much an infant perceives and understands of his surroundings, rather than examine his motor development. With the aid of these tests, Kagan has obtained results very different from those of researchers who have used standard infant tests. For example, the effect of social class is seen in the very first year of life, he reports. At sixteen weeks of age—not quite four months—children of parents of less than high-school education vocalize less. The effect is latent and subtle at four months, but absolutely clear at one year. Babies from lower social classes can't discriminate as well between similar stimuli, and they also vocalize less.

How can that be? I asked him. I had read that infants who lived in crowded homes with many people around them day and night, much noise and little privacy, received on the whole more stimulation than middle-class children during their first year of life. This was supposed to explain their high performance on tests of psychomotor development.

"It's the *distinctiveness* of the stimulation that's most important—not its sheer quantity," Kagan replied. "The best thing about the middle-class kid is that he's up in his room alone play-ing with his fingers. Then after an hour his mother comes in, leans over his crib, and says, 'Hello, Billy!' " Here Kagan clapped his hands to show the impact this must have. "That's it!" he exclaimed. "A single, distinctive stimulus—that's what you need. The other kids, who are surrounded by noise all the time, from TV and many voices, learn to 'tune it out' right in the living room. You don't learn anything in a Tower of Babel. The main question is, *Is the mother distinctive?*"

For the first-born child, the adult is the most distinctive stimu-lus around, Kagan pointed out. For a fifth-born, whose four older siblings continually poke, fuss, and vocalize into the crib, the caretaking adult is, of necessity, less distinctive; as a result, less attention will be paid to the adult. The fact that first-born children are nearly always more verbal, and generally have higher IQ's than their younger brothers or sisters, is directly related to this observation.

It follows that what is often termed "enrichment"—a hodge-podge of things to see, touch, and hear in an overstuffed class-room—is largely useless to slum children. Instead, said Kagan, people who plan such programs should provide single, distinctive stimuli, to be presented in a context of quiet. Culturally disad-vantaged children are not deprived of stimulation; they are deprived of distinctive stimulation.

What makes things seem distinctive to a child? Here Kagan urged a relativistic attitude: Both the context of the situation and the child's own level must be taken into account. To be truly distinctive, one needs to know a great deal about where the student stands. Teachers must start by observing their pupils as analytically as Piaget, and parents must learn new ways of per-ceiving their children.

Thus, parents can no longer afford their old insouciance about the first years of life. Besides listening with the third ear for evidence of emotional problems, they must now develop a fourth ear to hear the patterns of intellectual growth.

Like learning a new language, this will enrich their own lives, as well as help their children. Perhaps fathers stand to gain the most from this fourth ear. Until now, the first year of a child's life has usually held little interest for them. The period before the baby said his first word, or took his first step, has often seemed messy and unrewarding—the baby himself, incomprehensible. But if fathers can see exactly what is happening to their infants, trying to match each stage of development becomes an exciting game.

Even the selection of toys then takes on added meaning. As Bruner points out, letting toy manufacturers decide what toys should be available for children is like letting druggists decide what type of drugs should be given to patients off the street. Bruner would like to design toys based on what has been discovered about the early years—toys that are self-rewarding, giving children an opportunity to exercise new structures. "For example, things appear and disappear. Peek-a-boo games are quite extraordinary in their power. They can practically produce cardiac arrest! It's the drama of the object reappearing: Is it gone, or not gone? I operate on the assumption that the main source of growth is conflict. This may be an Old Testament view of things, but growth comes from suffering two systems that you can't put together. So this kind of game is the essence of what we have to do." In addition, Bruner has convinced Charles Eames to start designing crib mobiles that lead to a sequence of things. "Perhaps he can design a toy such that if you whack it on one side, it'll go 'ping,' and if you whack it on the other side, it'll go 'ping-ping,' but if you get it on the wrong side, it'll just go 'fff," muses Bruner. "This ought to produce excitement in the child! It would help him recognize that there are some sequences of behavior that lead somewhere, and others that don't."

Every human infant wants to go-go-go. The explorers of infancy are beginning to find out how each cognitive step leads to the next, and how to help the infant climb them. Tender loving care and mothering are not enough. Even the youngest infant also needs something interesting to do.

Chapter 10

THE HIDDEN CURRICULUM

IN LANGUAGE

A THREE-YEAR-OLD who cannot talk arouses grave concern, for good reasons. But the everyday miracle of a toddler's learning to speak tends to be taken for granted—though it is probably the most difficult intellectual accomplishment a human being is ever called upon to perform.

How do children do it? This question fascinates a new generation of psycholinguists and sociolinguists, who write scholarly dissertations about such childish forms of speech as "I digged a hole" or "Look at the sheeps!" Until recently, students of language focused on whatever they could measure easily—the size of young children's vocabulary, for example, or the length of their sentences. Today's crop of linguists is primarily interested in the process through which children reinvent the major rules of syntax—since nobody could teach toddlers these rules before they are able to speak.

Mistakes such as "I digged" seem particularly intriguing, for they could not be imitations of adult speech. Instead, they show that children as young as two or three apply complex rules of grammar which they have figured out by themselves.

A related question is how children's ways of thinking change after they have mastered speech. What have these youngsters learned, together with their new words and phrases? What is the "hidden curriculum" in language?

The linguists' findings so far mesh very neatly with Piaget's description of young children's intellectual development. At any stage of the game, says Piaget, the child has one characteristic way of viewing the world; at any stage of the game, say the linguists, the child's utterances have one particular degree of complexity—the same whether he speaks spontaneously or tries to imitate an adult. In both cases, the level reached by the child depends on what he has assimilated before, as well as on the quality of his present environment. But there is this difference: While motor skills and the ability to "conserve" are learned through contact with objects, language can be learned only by listening and responding to human beings.

When a child begins to speak—after the baby's babble and some grunts or sounds—he utters what the linguists call holophrases: single words ("Mummy," "see") or very short phrases that are used as one word ("gimme," "all gone"), defying grammatical analysis.

Then one fine day, around eighteen months of age, the child suddenly makes a two-word utterance that has a grammatical structure. He takes one of the holophrases and uses it as a pivot on which he can mount many other words ("See doggie" or "See light").

"At this particular point," says Bruner, "as far as I am concerned, he enters the human race as a speaker, because I think you can find examples of holophrastic utterances in higher primates, but you will never find combinatorial grammar.

"The rate at which the child operates on this pivot class is very striking. In the first week you usually get five or ten instances of the use of the combinatorial form; the second week it will jump to say seventy, and the next week to seven hundred. From there on out, it just explodes."

Listening to a child's first words and phrases becomes particularly enjoyable when one is attuned to this process. What holophrases does each child select, and why? Which does he use as pivots? At what stage do the combinations explode? One of my children, a very active little boy, preferred such verbs as "jump," "play," "go," "walk," "kiss," using these as pivots with the names of relatives, friends, and toys. The other one, when he was the same age, spent his time compiling lists of food: He would wake us up at 6 A.M. to ask, "D'you-wan' salt? D'you-wan' pepper? D'you-wan' sugar? D'you-wan' milk?"

Bruner cites the story of the child who watched his mother saying good-by to an aunt, and then declared, "All gone by-by." This is extraordinary because it is obviously not an imitation of adult grammar; it is entirely productive, Bruner comments. The child has formed a new combination entirely on his own, using the powerful tool of language. Later that day, the child had jam all over his hands. His mother took him to the bathroom to wash it off, and the child said, "All gone sticky"— another brilliant piece of combinatorial grammar in which the child brought things together which would not ordinarily be brought together.

The Center for Cognitive Studies has given increased attention to linguistics in the past few years. One of its members, social psychologist Dr. Roger Brown, recently made the first really detailed, longitudinal study of young children's language as it develops under normal circumstances in their own homes. His researchers spent at least two hours every week tape-recording the conversation of three first-born children—Adam, Eve, and Sara—and their mothers, from the time these children started putting two words together until they were speaking in complete sentences—a period of one or two years.

These tapes were analyzed by the staff and discussed at weekly seminars, which often led to additional experiments that had to be done immediately to be informative. Thus, when Dr. Brown could not answer whether two-year-old Adam really understood the difference between making a noun the subject or object of a sentence, a researcher was dispatched to Adam's house at once, bearing a toy duck. "Show us the duck pushing the boat," she asked Adam, who complied. "Now, show us the boat pushing the duck." Adam, the son of highly educated parents, went along with the game this time. But on other occasions he was less cooperative. In doubt as to whether he understood plurals, a researcher once asked him, "Which is right, 'two shoes' or 'two shoe'?" As recorded in the staid *Harvard Educational Review*: "His answer on that occasion, produced with explosive enthusiasm, was 'Pop goes the weasel!' " The article added dryly: "The two-year-old child does not make a perfectly docile experimental subject."

The dialogues between mother and child had a flavor of their own, the researchers pointed out. They differed from dialogues between adults, as well as from dialogues between children. The mother's sentences were short and simple—more grammatical than those casually used between adults, and longer than those used by children. For the most part, they were the kinds of sentences that Adam would produce a year later, noted Brown about Adam's mother's speech.

When Adam tried to repeat what his mother said, however, an interesting thing happened: He repeated it in telegraphese. For example: "Fraser will be unhappy" became "Fraser unhappy." "Mummy is going to have her soup" became "Mummy soup." These words were far from a random selection—the child systematically extracted from each sentence the words with the most information and distinctiveness, while preserving their original order. Yet his sentences were never more complicated than those he could produce spontaneously. Brown believes that this results not from limited memory, since the child may know hundreds of words, but rather from a limited programming ability; the child simply cannot plan sentences beyond a certain level of complexity.

Each stage of language development can thus be compared to a different program for the child's computer—his brain. His early programs are not only simpler, but different from the ones he uses later.

Researchers do not yet understand, however, just how these programs evolve—nor how they affect the child's general ability to think. Must the child first form mental images of things by manipulating these things, as Piaget implies, or will knowing their names help him identify them, as some linguists believe? Unlike the chicken-or-the-egg problem, this question has practical applications. For example, no matter how many objects a poor child has handled, he will be unable to compare quantities efficiently unless he understands the terms "more" and "less," "most" and "least."

A large number of psychologists, both in the United States and the Soviet Union, have shown that children learn more rapidly when they can name things or talk about problems as they go along. Verbal ability and intelligence are inseparable, they believe. Even those intelligence tests that are supposedly nonverbal really require children to verbalize—out loud or to themselves—before they can solve problems involving, for example, shapes which must be rotated or reversed.

In Russian experiments with children as young as one to two and a half, the toddlers who were told the name of the color red learned to find candy under a red cap much more easily than those who had no name for it; in fact, they required only one-third as many trials. They also remembered what they had learned much longer, and proved able to transfer their new learning to other circumstances—to find candy under a red box, a red cup, or a piece of red material—almost immediately, while the others could not.

Other Russian investigators told children to find a butterfly whose wings were like those of a butterfly they had been given. At first, the children could match the butterflies only by color, disregarding the patterns on the wings. But when one group was given verbal labels for the patterns ("spots," "stripes," "nets,") even its youngest members learned to match the butterfly wings accurately and speedily, while the control group could not. Without names for the patterns, they seemed unable even to see them.

> I have forgotten the word I intended to say,
> and my thought, unembodied,
> returns to the realm of shadows. . . .

With these lines from a Russian poem by Osip Mandelstam, another Russian, Lev Vygotsky, underscores the importance of words in mental processes. Vygotsky, a psychologist, died at an early age and never saw the publication of his best-known book, *Thought and Language*. This appeared in the Soviet Union in 1934, a few months after his death. Although it was banned by the Soviet Government two years after publication, it remained a strong influence on a whole generation of Russian psychologists, many of whom are primarily interested in education. It reappeared in Russia in 1956, but did not make the American scene until 1962, when an English-language edition was published by the Massachusetts Institute of Technology. Since then it has proved increasingly influential among American psychologists and educators as well as linguists.

Vygotsky's main point is that the role of language changes as the child grows up. At first it serves a largely social function

—to express the child's immediate needs or moods. But eventually language becomes internalized as an instrument for thought. Then the child uses language even when he does not speak— a kind of language which Vygotsky calls inner speech, speech for oneself, as opposed to speech for others.

The preschoolers who seem to think aloud, in an often strange-sounding, disconnected sort of monologue, are at an intermediate stage, during which, according to Vygotsky, their voiced "egocentric" speech fulfills the functions of inner speech.

To illustrate how the young child's egocentric speech may alter the course of his activities, Vygotsky tells of an accident that occurred during one of his experiments: "A child of five and a half was drawing a streetcar when the point of his pencil broke. He tried, nevertheless, to finish the circle of a wheel, pressing down on the pencil very hard, but nothing showed on the paper except a deep colorless line. The child muttered to himself, 'It's broken,' put aside the pencil, took water colors instead, and began drawing a broken streetcar after an accident, continuing to talk to himself from time to time about the change in his picture. The child's accidentally provoked egocentric utterance so manifestly affected his activity that it is impossible to mistake it for a mere by-product, an accompaniment not interfering with the melody."

With younger children, says Vygotsky, egocentric speech marks the end result, or a turning point, of an activity. As they grow older, they use such speech at the middle, and finally at the beginning of an activity. It then takes on a directing, planning function, and raises the child's acts to the level of purposeful behavior. This resembles the well-known sequence according to which a small child draws first, then decides what it is that he has drawn, points out Vygotsky. At a slightly older age, he names his drawing when it is half done; and, finally, he decides beforehand what he will draw.

As the function of speech changes, so does its quality. Vygotsky reports that he taught a mute child the words "table," "chair," "bureau," "couch," "shelves" and so on, without much difficulty. The term "furniture," however, proved too hard to grasp. Thus, for Vygotsky, the appearance of the first generalized concept, such as "furniture" or "clothes," is as significant a symptom of progress as the first meaningful word.

Direct teaching of concepts is impossible and fruitless, he believes. But instruction in mathematics, language, or any subject which activates large areas of consciousness certainly promotes the child's total mental growth. A child who has learned to write is a different child, with sharpened memory, attention, and thinking. He thus rises to a higher level of speech development.

The only good kind of instruction is that which marches ahead of development, and leads it, Vygotsky declares. It must be aimed not so much at the ripe as at the ripening functions. He also points out that during certain sensitive periods in a child's life, instruction which might have little effect earlier or later may radically affect the course of his intellectual growth.

Vygotsky is an activist. He believes that instruction can change a child's verbal development, which in turn directs his thinking.

A very different view of the role of language comes from a British sociologist, Dr. Basil Bernstein. On a recent American lecture tour, Bernstein started on a negative note: "There is nothing I can do that can change the effects of social class on children."

Bernstein teaches the sociology of education at the University of London, where he has pioneered in the study of how class differences affect the selection of linguistic codes. Children learn either "restricted" or "elaborated" speech codes, according to their place in the social structure, he believes—and these codes make a mockery of the so-called equality of opportunity in education.

The child who learns a restricted linguistic code from his lower-working-class parents also learns, says Bernstein, that nothing really important is ever transmitted by language. In his family, the strongest messages take nonverbal forms: gestures, intonations, actions. Language is reserved for routinized and predictable messages. Bernstein compares this situation to life in the Army, where "your role is so prescribed that the only way you can signal your personal difference is the angle at which you wear your cap, or put your tongue in your cheek." Speech in a restricted-code family also reflects a common cultural identity: that of a social group with little decision-making power, with little variety in its environment, and whose main work task is physical manipulation or docility, rather than symbolic operations.

To control her children, the mother in a restricted-code family does not talk about their actions or investigate their motives, but simply announces general rules which must be obeyed. Suppose she takes a child to visit his ailing grandfather, who doesn't shave much, and whose chin is full of bristles, suggests Bernstein. She might then say, "When you go to Grandpa, I want none of your nonsense—you kiss him!" In the same situation, the mother in an elaborated-code family might say, "I know you don't want to kiss Grandpa [thus giving the child at least the semblance of a choice in the matter], but it makes him so happy when you do—please kiss him!" The first is an example of positional control, in which the child must do certain things because of his status. The second is personal control, which Bernstein calls downright blackmail—but at least the rule is achieved by the child. He learns the role of regulator; he learns the consequences of his actions; and a whole order of learning is made available to him.

Elaborated codes reflect a milieu in which people express their uniqueness through language, says Bernstein. Since language carries the really important messages, these codes require a high level of vocabulary selection and syntactical organization—the very elaboration that also makes it possible to express abstract thoughts.

Depending on their linguistic codes, children will have different responses to the same educational opportunities, Bernstein maintains. They will develop very differently, despite the same potential. For the child from a restricted-code family, school will be an experience of extreme cultural discontinuity; it may even seem irrelevant to real life, leaving him puzzled, bewildered, alienated. This does not disvalue his communication system—it has a vast potential, he emphasizes; it just happens not to be terribly helpful if you want to join the rat race. Jazz and prize fighting are examples of the complex codes used by people who filter their experience through nonverbal channels.

"My thesis," says Bernstein, "is that if you change the culture, you change the language." But he adds, "Never have I said what should be done; I have a purely theoretical orientation, with limited evidence based upon studies of middle-class and working-class children." It is, obviously, much more difficult to change a child's total milieu than to provide a few hours of instruction.

"What are the applications of your theory to the education of the disadvantaged?" someone asked after one of Bernstein's New York lectures. "How can we actually use your model?"

Bernstein sighed. "Use it with love!" he replied. He deplored the fact that the intervention movement in the United States, a great bureaucracy built on rather limited experience, is in the hands of psychologists. He would want to draw into this field thinkers and workers in sociology, anthropology, and other social sciences. "My own view is that the notion of 'deficit' is inappropriate," he said. "It turns the social scientist into a plumber: You see the child in terms of something he hasn't got! This loses track of the child's vital experience. It is only one way of looking at a situation, and while it is a valid way, it is dangerous when it is the only way."

Whatever point of view one prefers, however—that of the linguists, of Vygotsky, or of Bernstein—one fact emerges with clarity: the enormous importance of the mother's speech patterns. "Language," says Bernstein, "is a tool that changes you as you use it." If there is a small child around, the language that he hears others use changes him even more.

Mothers increasingly are seen as teachers or "programmers of input," and the primary input is language. Different kinds of input produce different strategies for processing information— different cognitive styles in the child. He may either learn to consider consequences, to reflect, to select from a wide range of alternatives, or he may learn to do what he is told without hesitation. The hidden curriculum of the home, in the sociologists' phrase, is transmitted primarily through language.

At the University of Chicago, psychologist Robert D. Hess studied the teaching styles of four groups of urban Negro mothers as they spoke to their four-year-old children. One group (middle-class) came from college-educated families; the next (upper-lower-class) represented high-school-educated skilled workers, and the last two (lower-lower) represented either unskilled workers with no more than elementary-school education, or families on public assistance. So far as could be judged, the love and affection between mother and child were approximately the same in all groups. The mothers were then asked to teach their children how to sort out a small number of toys, while a tape recorder took down what they said.

The middle-class mothers gave their children enough information and guidance to allow them to proceed on their own. "All right, Susan," began one mother, "this board is the place where we put the little toys; first of all, you're supposed to learn how to place them according to color. Can you do that? The things that are all the same color you put in one section; in the second section you put another group of colors; and in the third section you put the last group of colors. Can you do that? Or would you like to see me do it first?" "*I* want to do it!" responded her child immediately.

Relying more on nonverbal communication, an upper-lower-class mother began as follows: "Now, I'll take them all off the board; now you put them all back on the board. What are these?" Her child replied, "A truck." "All right," said the mother, "just put them right here; put the other one right here; all right, put the other one there." She gave directions, but never explained the task.

A lower-lower-class mother was even less explicit, introducing the task as follows: "I've got some chairs and cars. Do you want to play the game?" Her child did not respond, so she continued, "O.K. What's this?" "A wagon?" asked the child. "Hm?" questioned the mother. "A wagon?" repeated the child doubtfully. "This is not a wagon," said the mother. "What's this?" The conversation continued in this ineffectual way, with the child receiving no clues at all to the nature of the problem he faced. Naturally, he was unable to solve it.

In trying to predict the performance of children in various tests, Hess found that the mother's teaching style was often a better predictor than either the child's IQ, the mother's IQ, or social class. The meaning of deprivation, he concluded, thus seems to be a *deprivation of meaning* in the early cognitive relationships between mother and child. Since the child's central task is to deal with the environment so that life makes sense, such deprivation is a major handicap.

Perhaps because it is so difficult to translate the new theories about language development into educational programs, few people have tried it. One who did, Courtney Cazden, of Harvard University, came up with unexpected results.

A former first-grade teacher, Mrs. Cazden wanted to find out what caused the tremendous differences she had noticed between middle-class and working-class children at the age of six. To do so, she worked with Roger Brown on the study of Adam, Eve, and Sara. This seemed to show that young children learned most about language when their parents expanded what they said. For example, when a child made a telegraphic utterance such as "Mummy lunch," the parent responded with the nearest complete sentence—"Mummy is having her lunch"—adding only the parts which the child had omitted.

For her doctoral dissertation, Mrs. Cazden decided to try out systematic expansion for forty minutes a day with a group of three-year-old Negro children from a crowded day-care center. She planned to compare their progress with that of two other groups of three-year-olds from the same center, one of whom would receive no special treatment, while the other would be given a chance to hear "modeling"—well-formed sentences that were deliberately *not* expansion. She was quite sure that the children who had the expansion would do best of all. To her surprise, at the end of three months the group that had had modeling did better than either of the others on six measures of language development.

This led her to take another look at what actually happened during modeling, and she soon found that something quite interesting was involved: If a child says, "Dog bark" when a dog is barking, the expanding adult can say little more than "Yes, the dog is barking," she pointed out. But in order to maintain a reasonable conversation during modeling, the adult must contribute a related idea: "Yes, he's mad at the kitty" or "Yes, but he won't bite." Thus, focusing on grammar limited the conversation to the child's own grammatical elements and ideas; by contrast, focusing on ideas led beyond the presumed meaning of the child and also introduced more varied grammatical elements. She decided to call this method "expatiation" rather than plain modeling. Her conclusion: Language that is impoverished is harder—not easier—to learn.

In this she agreed with the Russian experimenters who tried to find out whether small children would learn the word "doll" more easily when it was used repetitively or in different ways. Five twenty-month-old tots were shown a particular doll a total of 1,500 times over several months while the experimenter used only three phases about it: "Here is a doll," "Take the doll," or "Give me the doll." Another five children of the same age were shown the doll an equal number of times while the experimenter used *thirty* different phrases about it, such as "Rock the doll," "Feed the doll," "Look for the doll," and so on. The total amount of speech they heard was the same in both cases. Then both groups of children were asked to pick a doll from a large number of different dolls and toys, to see which had a better grasp of the concept "doll." The children in the first group picked out dolls, but sometimes picked out other toys as well. Those in the second group, however, picked out only dolls.

If this is true as early as the age of twenty months, just after what Piaget calls the take-off point into abstract thought, it goes a long way toward explaining the differences between slum children and middle-class children by the age of five. Lower-class parents seldom "expatiate" on their children's ideas, and their language offers very little variety.

Both these Russian and American experiments, limited as they are, seem to tell parents not to be overly afraid of complexity in their speech. Be interesting to your little child, they imply, and for goodness' sake don't talk down! You may then be rewarded by your child's rich and poetic use of language, as well as by his developing intellect.

Mrs. Cazden refers to Adam's comment, "Coffee dancing," as

the cream swirls in his mother's cup, as a delightful example of three-year-old creativity. Any observant and talkative parent can contribute his own samples of preschoolers' poetic speech.

For similar reasons, reading books to children before they even seem able to understand language—from the age of one—is extremely important. This is common practice in middle-class homes, but almost unheard-of among poorer families. When lower-class mothers were paid to read aloud to their infants for at least ten minutes a day, in a recent experiment, their children forged ahead of a control group and showed significant differences in all phases of speech by twenty months of age.

It is easy to predict that the first-born child of college-educated parents will be a very verbal child, says Mrs. Cazden, because he will hear a lot of varied talk and have more contact with his parents than any subsequent siblings. But it is much more difficult to isolate the critical factors in this relationship, or work out ways to introduce similar practices into lower-class homes. Furthermore, what's good for the middle-class infant and toddler at home may be totally inappropriate for the slum child at school much later, at the age of four or five. It may also be inappropriate for the middle-class child in school, because it is too repetitious.

The real challenge is that language develops so rapidly. The hidden curriculum in language does its work early, revealing itself only by its products. By eighteen or twenty months of age, certain processes have been set in motion that determine a major part of the child's future intellectual development unless his environment is drastically changed. When something goes wrong, it may not be detected until it is too late.

An equally invisible but speedy process is at work in connection with reading.

Chapter 11

EARLY READING

"Jimmy can read any book he wants," brags one father. And he adds: "He just taught himself." In some middle-class neighborhoods, this is the latest status symbol: having a child who can read by the age of four or five *without anybody having taught him*—at least in theory. Naturally, the other parents are green with envy. Some claim to feel sorry for the poor child, whose parents must have put so much pressure on him and whose emotional development will surely suffer. Others declare that it won't make any difference in the long run—it will all wash out after a few years in school.

Early reading arouses violent opinions. Yet everyone, particularly parents, remains vulnerable. Perhaps, after all, the other parents or experts are right? Perhaps it *is* good to read early—or, perhaps it will harm the child later on. Should reading be taught in kindergarten? Should it be taught at home? And if so, *how?*

The experts manage to make parents feel guilty if they do teach their youngsters to read, and guilty if they don't.

"Don't try to teach him letters at home," urges the typical nursery-school or kindergarten teacher; "he won't be 'ready' to read until he is at least six years old." When a child in their classes already knows how to read, they carefully ignore this ability. Meanwhile, the other children in the class have no opportunity to play with letters—there are none in the standard equipment of blocks, arts and crafts, trucks and dolls—though parents who ask whether the school teaches reading are usually told that the children learn to read through playing. At most, they may get reading-readiness exercises; for example, a picture of three cats in a row looking in one direction, and one cat (to be circled) looking in the opposite direction.

The kindergarten teacher in my son's school deliberately avoids teaching the children to read. Unlike many other teachers, she has high regard for the five-year-old intellect and believes her pupils could learn easily—"but then they'd be *miserable* in first grade!" she explains. As a compromise, she shows her class some consonants on a chart during the spring semester, when these middle-class children are nearly six and almost reading anyway. She is a vibrant, warm, handsome woman whom my child adores. "I *let* her think she's teaching me the letters, because it makes her happy," he told me one day.

While traditional teachers try to hold back on reading, aggressive promoters play on parental fears.

"Loser!" taunts an ad in a Sunday newspaper. "He's bright. He's cute. He's getting love and affection, and exactly the right amounts of Spock and vitamins. He's getting everything—except the one thing that will mean the difference a few years from now, between loving school and hating it. . . . He isn't learning how to read. . . . Right now, you can teach your baby to read—beginning at only two years of age!"

This pitch leads to an order form for a book that will tell how to condition your baby so he recognizes some common words, such as "toes." When the baby points to the right word, you must "be delighted and make a great fuss. Tell the child he is very good and very bright. Tell him that you love him very much. It is wise to hug him and to caress him," write the authors, blithely advising mothers to give their love (or to withhold it) according to how well their babies perform—an attitude that most psychologists abhor. The authors add that, with just a little more effort, mothers can begin this training when the baby is only eighteen months old or, "if you are very clever, as early as ten months."

Both types of pressure are directed at middle-class parents— the very people who generally teach their children some elements of reading anyway, regardless of the current fashion in experts or advice. They do this because they can't help it; they naturally tell their preschoolers something about letters and sounds as they answer questions about books, street signs, or labels. Since their whole world is surrounded by language, both written and spoken, their children take it in somewhat haphazardly through all their pores.

Occasionally some child who has been exposed to such information for years will put the pieces together and suddenly learn to read by himself. More often, children learn from their older brothers and sisters. Since neither their parents nor their teachers deliberately teach reading, however, the bulk of middle-class children cannot read before they enter first grade—but they are close enough to this skill to make the most of whatever the first grade has to offer. Regardless of the schools' inefficient teaching methods, these children seldom become reading problems.

Waiting until the age of six and then being taught ineffectively often proves disastrous for the children of poverty, however. Since they do poorly on first-grade reading-readiness tests— perhaps the most class-bound tests in existence—they sink to the bottom of the class right from the start. There the teacher gives them even fewer sight-words to memorize than to the other children. From then on, they may never catch up. They cannot compete with their middle-class schoolmates; they cannot please their teachers; they cannot begin to cope with what is expected of them. Only a few youngsters succeed in overcoming such odds. The rest—even those from loving and stable homes—fall by the wayside, joining the vast pool of functional illiterates and dropouts.

The teachers who are honest with themselves know this—and find it intolerable. I had a glimpse of what their life can be like when I spoke to a rather desperate young woman who teaches first grade in a poor section of New Jersey. Only one-third of the thirty children in her class could "read" at all, she told me; that is, only one-third understood, after much drill in putting their lips together at the symbol for "m," that placing "m" before "at" will produce "mat." They knew "at," she explained, because it comes after "look" in their primer. She taught whole words, not letter sounds. The children were supposed to learn the words that appeared in the primer—"go," "look at," "come," and so on —without any explanation of the letters that made them up.

"They're very eager to come forward; they wave their hands, they want to learn, it seems," the young teacher said. "But when I call on them, they'll say any old word, because they simply don't know." To arouse their interest, she had tried asking each child, in turn, what word he'd like to have as his very own, hoping that if they picked a word that really meant something to them they would remember it better. But to her disappointment, the children could think of no words besides "come" or "look"—the very words they had seen in the primer. Apparently they did not even realize that what they spoke all day *was* words.

Her instructions were to teach the children "initial consonants." This she planned to do, teaching consonant sounds one by one and hoping to get through many of them by the end of the year, though she did not really believe she would make much headway. She would not even attempt to teach vowels—this seemed too complicated in English. Nor would the children be taught to recombine the letters of the words they already knew, to make other words, since she believed that teaching the sounds of the letters alone would mean nothing to them.

In fact, she was at a loss for what to do with these children, except ask to have them tested—that is, have their names put on a list. But if they tested above 60 IQ, they wouldn't qualify for any special classes (of which there weren't enough anyway). Their IQ's actually averaged between 80 and 90. Most of the children in her class had been through kindergarten; yet she still had to teach them number concepts; when she asked for four jars, for example, she had to teach the child to bring four and not three; then she would write the number on the blackboard.

Some of the children were repeating first grade, and most would have to repeat it at the end of this year, she said. As a last resort, she had recently called up a friend who teaches retarded children in Minnesota. Over the telephone, the friend had advised her to try kindergarten books—books with pictures only, no words— and she had followed this advice. "The kids love these books— it's something they can do," she said unhappily. "They figure out which picture does not belong on the page, and so on. This way, perhaps if they do all the kindergarten stuff okay this year, they'll be ready for first grade when they repeat it next year." But the second-grade teachers already had problems of the same sort in their classes. Meanwhile, she was worried about not covering any of the stuff she was supposed to cover this year. She had nobody to discuss the problem with. No official advice was available, and there was only one psychologist for the entire school system.

With this kind of school to look forward to, the single most useful thing that can be done for culturally disadvantaged youngsters is undoubtedly to teach them to read—by other methods—before they enter school. For, quite obviously, reading is the key to all the rest of their school subjects, and the present system works only with children who have learned its fundamentals before they enter first grade.

Yet the Head Start program, like many other preschool programs, discourages attempts at teaching young children to read. "I don't know why our nation is so fixated on reading," says Dr. Keith Osborne, a psychologist who is educational consultant to Head Start. "It's a *tool*—why do we make it a god? Perhaps the god should be getting-along-with-people, rather than reading. If you do teach kids to read early, so what? You may get a child of three who knows how to read, but still doesn't get along with others." Head Start should make up for areas of deprivation, he says, but not be concerned with starting school eight weeks earlier—like teaching children to read.

This comfortable viewpoint is typical of those who believe in the nebulous theory of reading readiness, and then apply it indiscriminately to all children, regardless of their social background.

"Your child may be ready to read at five. Some few children are. Your child may show that he is ready at six. Some six-year-olds—not all, by any means—are all set to go. But your youngster may not be really eager to work with a book until he is seven or eight," writes the highly respected James L. Hymes, Jr., professor of child development and education at the University of Maryland, and a member of Head Start's planning committee. "Inside of each of us there is a timetable. Our own personal rate of growing. . . . You have to grow muscles that make your eyes move in a certain direction. Your eyes have to develop so you can see things at a certain distance. You have to grow the nerves that will tell you the difference between a 'c' and an 'o' or 'e.' And all of these you grow at your own sweet rate. When your child is ready you will know it."

In other words, the burden of proof is on the child—he must *show* that he is ready to read. How is he to show this? Dr. Hymes explains: "He will ask you over and over, 'What is that word?' [though most slum children don't even know what a word is, and have nobody to ask]. He will stop you time and again when you are reading—'Show me where it says . . .' [though slum children have no one who'll read to them, and thus no one to stop]. He will eagerly tell you, "That says *Slow* . . . That says *Wheaties*'" [which again presupposes that the child had a tutor who pointed out these words to him in the first place].

Continuing his "let-them-eat-cake" argument in a Public Affairs pamphlet entitled "*Three to Six*," Dr. Hymes concludes: "You couldn't keep him from crawling . . . not when he was one month but when he had grown enough to crawl. You couldn't keep him from going up stairs . . . not when he was six months but when he had grown enough to climb. You couldn't keep him from talking . . . not when he was ten months but when he had grown enough to jabber. The same will hold true with reading." If it did, there would be no illiterates anywhere in the world.

There seems no reason to believe that American slum children are any less ready to read than the Italian slum children who regularly learned to read at the age of four or five in Maria Montessori's Casa dei Bambini. Nor are American children less ready than all the English schoolchildren who, to this day, start learning to read when they enter Infant School at five, or earlier. Nor are they more primitive than the Maori children whom Sylvia Ashton-Warner, the author of *Spinster* and *Teacher*, taught to read in New Zealand at five. The whole idea of reading readiness is so vague, in fact, that it has been said really to mean the readiness of the teacher to let the child begin.

Leaving aside the arguments about readiness, there are certain real advantages to early reading for all children, though disadvantaged children stand to benefit more from it. Besides giving the child greater mastery over his environment—he can make use of street signs, labels, and a variety of guideposts—reading opens up a world of information for him, and as he gets more "input" he tends to reach a higher level of development, which will make future learning easier. He also gains access to a wealth of literature—nursery tales, fairy tales, adventure, fantasy—from which to pick what is just right for him at any stage. By the time he enters first grade, he need not be limited to the inane, deliberately repetitious stories in his Dick and Jane readers ("Here, Spot. Here, Spot. Come here, Spot") or the other miserable stuff to which first-graders are usually condemned because of their restricted sight-reading vocabulary. Even third-graders who are doing well in school can seldom read more than one-tenth of their own speaking and listening vocabulary. Nor can they write their own thoughts with ease. What they have learned is wordiness and fuzzy thinking—and, all too often, a violent distaste for books.

When reading instruction is begun early, it often provides the only clue to some serious visual disabilities—lumped under the term dyslexia—which can be largely corrected if caught in time, but otherwise can poison the child's life. An estimated 10 percent of children with normal intelligence suffer from handicaps in perception, failing to process with sufficient accuracy the information received from their eyes and ears. Sometimes they cannot tell left from right, or up from down. Sometimes, despite otherwise normal hearing, they scramble sounds that are somewhat alike. In the past, psychologists concentrated on making the most of what functioned normally in these children, but today the trend is to train the senses that are weak—and for this it is essential to start early.

Unfortunately, since they teach neither reading nor writing, nursery and kindergarten teachers usually don't find out about these handicaps. The problem shows up only when the children start going to school. "An ordinary medical exam is not enough, for medical doctors are not geared to looking for this; they don't even have the right tests," says a psychologist who specializes in remedial work with children who have reading problems. "You need to make a full profile of the child's abilities. This ought to be done in every kindergarten or nursery school, but it never is done."

By the time children are referred to her by teachers or psychiatrists, it is sometimes impossible to teach such things as vowel sounds—the children don't hear the differences. "The more intelligent these children are, the more they suffer from it," she says. "So you get emotional difficulties on top of it all." Yet at an earlier age they might have been trained successfully. Many of the exercises that have been worked out for this purpose are based on Montessori techniques. The idea is to use as many pathways to the brain as possible—to make the children see, hear, and feel specific shapes or sounds of increasing complexity. With early detection and a year or two of intensive training, most of these children can be prepared to handle a regular school program.

Far from running into problems when they enter school, as so many parents fear, children who learn to read early maintain their lead in reading achievement over the years, according to a longitudinal study by Professor Dolores Durkin, of the University of Illinois College of Education. She carefully compared thirty early readers (children who learned to read before the age of six) with thirty children who learned later. The two groups had the same average IQ and the same first-grade teacher. By the end of the third grade, the early readers were still an average of one year ahead.

When Professor Durkin studied the children's parents she found that they differed most strikingly in their conception of their own role during their children's preschool years. All the parents of the early readers had noticed the children's interest in reading by the age of four, all had responded by identifying letters, numbers, words, and sounds for them, answering their questions, discussing the meanings of words, and so on. On the other hand, the parents of the children who learned to read later generally believed that reading should be taught only at school by a trained person. They said such things as: "The system today is different. Reading is so important that it should be taught properly, so that no complications arise" or "I've always been told to let the school take care of the reading." One mother stated, "We have followed a strict hands-off policy. . . . We have stayed out of forbidden territory." Another said, "When she asked about words, I just told her she'd learn to read when she got to first grade. . . . I didn't want to teach her anything that might cause problems later on." "I'm not an aggressive mother. Mine are normal, intelligent children. They'll learn in school. . . . I don't want to mix them up," commented another parent.

Some of the mothers of children who did not read early had tried tutoring them when the children had made no special request for it. This had not lasted long. One reason for its failure, according to Dr. Durkin, is that "young children are more responsive to help with reading that is the consequence of their questions rather than of parents' ambition, insecurity, or whatever else leads them to try to teach children to read." Another reason was simply the busy lives of these mothers. By contrast, she noted, not one mother of an early reader ever used the word "busy" in talking about herself. Instead, several mothers described their children's questions and observations as so interesting that sharing in them was sheer joy, as one mother put it.

Both this study, which was made in New York City over a three-year period, and an earlier study made by Dr. Durkin in California over a six-year period support the notion that an early start in reading has most value for the slow learner. Although the high-IQ children who did not learn to read early never quite caught up with those of similar IQ's who did, the gap between them narrowed over the years. However, low-IQ children who had learned to read early kept their full two- or three-year lead over equally low-IQ children who had not.

The few nursery schools and kindergartens that did want to help children read early have had little to choose from in way of methods until recently. Unless they adopted total systems like Montessori's, which taught reading almost incidentally, there were only the same tired techniques which had had such limited success in first grade. Right now there seems to be a renaissance in this field, however, with linguists, programmers, specialists in perception, and experienced teachers, all lending a hand.

Among the more effective methods developed so far are various forms of programming and the use of Pitman's Initial Training Alphabet, usually called ITA.

Each of these tackles the inconsistencies of the English language in an original manner, so as to make written English appear logical to the child. Each allows the child to proceed at his own pace—a great advantage over the lock-step organization of most first grades. Each provides the teacher with a useful record of the child's progress and difficulties, making it much easier for her to monitor his work. And each has been used successfully with children of kindergarten age—though mostly those from middle-class homes.

Unlike some languages whose letters nearly always represent a single sound, such as Italian, English is discouragingly irregular. The letter "o," for example, is pronounced four different ways in "bone, one, gone, done." The sound of letter "i" is spelled differently in "aisle, height, choir, eye, pie, cry, sigh, buy, guide, island" and twelve other ways. It defies logic.

These inconsistencies help to explain why the look-say, or whole-word, method has dominated the teaching of reading in American schools since 1925. The look-say method requires children to recognize, or memorize, whole words at a glance, rather than read them by means of the letters that make them up. It was attacked by Rudolf Flesch a decade ago in his fiery best-seller *Why Johnny Can't Read.* "We have decided to forget that we write with letters, and learn to read English as if it were Chinese," Flesch charged. Before the invention of the alphabet 3,500 years ago, he pointed out, there was only picture writing—a picture of an ox meant "ox." This meant that one had to learn a different symbol for every word in the language. The great advantage of the alphabet was that one needed to learn only a limited number of letters with which one could write everything. Yet American primers and teachers insisted that children learn words by rote, leaving them unfit to read any word they had not met before. Flesch advocated a return to strict "phonics," which drilled children on the sound of each letter before letting them read words or sentences, as the only solution to America's reading problem.

The fierce battle between look-say and phonics has simmered down in recent years, with most teachers agreeing—at least in principle—that reading is best taught by a combination of both. In practice, however, teachers tend to follow their primers and readers, most of which are still based on look-say.

Look-say primers use words which seem easy because they are short and common, but which obey no rules. Such words make up roughly 15 percent of the English language: "come," "laugh," "said," and so on. The Sullivan Programmed Reading Series, a good example of programming techniques, concentrates on words that are completely regular. Care is taken not to expose the child to irregularities until he has fully mastered the regular sound value for each symbol. Thus, the first books in the series present the letter "a" only when it has a short sound, as in "mat." This sound is repeated at least one thousand times before the long sound for "a," as in "gate," is introduced.

Although no teaching machine is used, the twenty-one books in the Sullivan series resemble teaching machines in their small steps and rigid sequences. The child fills in blanks in pencil and corrects his own mistakes. If he responds, he is learning, says Dr. M. W. Sullivan, a programmer, linguist, and former teacher who developed the series, together with programmer Cynthia Dee Buchanan. Sullivan, now thirty-seven years old, has his own firm in Los Altos, California, which produces many kinds of programmed materials for schools.

Before any child can start on the books, however, he must be taught certain basics by the teacher: the names of the letters; how to print capital and small letters; the fact that letters stand for sounds; the fact that groups of letters form words; the principle that letters are read from left to right; the sounds to associate with the letters "a, f, m, n, p, t, th, and i,"; and the sight-words "yes" and "no"—quite an ambitious program for children from disadvantaged homes.

Only after the child has learned how to read the sentence "I am an ant" does the Programmed Reading method really come into its own. The child then sees the drawing of an ant in his primer and circles one of two words: "man" and "ant." He sees two men—one tall and skinny, one very fat—and circles one of them as he reads "I am a fat man." He learns to complete words in which a letter is missing and to cover the answers on the left-hand margin with a slider. Why should he cheat? That would deprive him of the pleasure of finding out that he was correct, as he is at least 95 percent of the time.

When he has finished the primer and passed a test, he can proceed to Book 1, for which the teacher's constant help is no longer necessary. From then on, he raises his hand for help only when he has finished one of the tests, which occur every fifteen pages, or when something particularly difficult stumps him. Freed of the need to present rote materials, the teacher can spend all her time doing individual tutoring.

Meanwhile, the child is reading real stories, not the usual pap. When Sullivan did a little market research, with children rather than with the experts, he discovered that the last things children wanted to read about were Daddy, Mommy, Teacher, the characters usually included in their story world, he says. They wanted animals and concrete things and much more meaningful subjects than those usually offered them. They did not even like the bland art style of traditional readers, preferring simple line drawings and bold colors, as in cartoons. The Programmed Reading books therefore contain riddles, poems, and fables, as well as a good deal of science, illustrated with lively drawings. The last books in the series include a long fantasy-adventure and tales about the heroes of Greek mythology.

Between twenty and thirty schools have tried out Programmed Reading with kindergarten children since 1961. At the Corte Madera School, a public elementary school in prosperous Portola Valley, California, kindergarten children took about three months to get through the Prereading Program, working with cards, slates, and alphabet charts fifteen minutes a day. Then they went on to the Primer and Book 1. By the end of the kindergarten year, they were well into Book 3, reading at a level that is supposed to correspond to the beginning of the second grade.

"Should these materials be used with kindergarten children?" I asked Programmed Reading's coauthor, Cynthia Buchanan, "That's what we would prefer," she replied. If kindergarten children would at least start with the sound-symbol relationships and go into Book 1, they would be in good shape to advance rapidly in first grade, she said. However, the program has not yet been tested with disadvantaged children of kindergarten age. At the first-grade level, children from the slums have experienced some difficulty with it.

An entirely different way of coping with the irregularities of the English language is to eliminate them. This Sir James Pitman, an English publisher, has tried to do with his Initial Training Alphabet (ITA). Sir James simply decreed that English shall be regular—and invented eighteen new letters to make it so. Thus, each symbol represents only one sound. Instead of learning upper- and lower-case letters of the twenty-six letter alphabet—a total of forty-three separate symbols—the beginner learns a forty-four-letter alphabet, in which capitals differ from lower-case letters only in size, and each letter says exactly what it means. Ingeniously, many of the augmentations, or new symbols, look like two familiar letters joined together: "æ," for example, represents the long sound of "a," while "a" represents the short sound; "œ" stands for the long sound of "o," and "o" for the short. These symbols are designed to make the child's eventual transition from ITA to the conventional alphabet as easy as possible.

The beauty of ITA is that once a child has mastered its forty-four symbols, he can read anything written in this alphabet and write anything he wishes, phonetically. Thus, creative writing can start almost immediately—the child is free.

Bernard Shaw had wished to free all Englishmen in this way by making English spelling completely phonetic and consistent. He urged such a reform in his will and appointed Sir James his executor. The grandson of Isaac Pitman, inventor of Pitman shorthand, Sir James had long been interested in codes and in language. Until the late 1950's he remained a supporter of the Simplified Spelling Society. But then he decided that a logical *initial* alphabet for beginning readers would serve much the same purpose as a permanent reform of English spelling, and would also stand a much greater chance of success. In 1961 the Ministry of Education gave him permission to carry out a large research project with ITA and children as young as four or five. This experiment is still in progress, but by March of 1964 the Minister of Education had enough evidence to announce his support for the project because of its success.

Now ITA is used to teach reading to nearly one-tenth of all British beginners. British children start learning to read no later than at five years of age. Some, in Wales, start as early as three, when their mothers bring them to Infant Schools so the parents can go off to work. One of the most interesting results of the experiment with ITA has been that the four-year-olds who are taught by this method make just as much progress during the first year as those who are five.

England's Prince Andrew did so well with ITA, which he started learning when he was four, that Prince Philip recently wrote to President Johnson, urging him to look into this method. Princess Margaret's four-year-old son, Viscount Linley, also learned to read this way with the group of friends making up his class at Buckingham Palace.

Though the British started this system, it remained for ITA's American supporters to go the whole way and write entirely new books for children in the augmented alphabet, rather than just translate the primers and readers based on the look-say method. Translating the old Dick-and-Jane readers into the new alphabet seemed as wasteful to the Pitman Publishing Corp., American affiliate of Pitman's in London, as to invent the airplane and then run it on the ground because of our familiarity with automobiles. Breaking loose from word lists and white suburban homes, this firm then published a set of readers on such subjects as dinosaurs, spacemen, deep-sea divers, and igloos.

A growing number of American schools have used ITA with first-graders, kindergarteners, and even four-year-olds, since 1963. Transition to the ordinary alphabet— which most teachers feared would be a problem—has taken place without difficulty, as long as the children stayed in the school long enough to see it through. The quickest youngsters who started ITA in first grade made the transition to ordinary spelling around the middle of the year; the slower ones waited until they reached second grade; the most disadvantaged did not make it until the end of second grade, but by then they read at least at grade level in the standard alphabet, and several read well above it.

All these children showed unusual interest in creative writing. In some schools the year's supply of paper was exhausted within three months as the children kept writing stories by themselves. One boy produced a 105-page book. They wrote in full sentences, revealing their problems and joys to the teachers, some of whom commented that they had gained a better understanding of their pupils' world.

The method also made it easier to correct children's errors of speech. When a little boy wrote, "I woto school" instead of "I walk to school," for example, he showed his teacher that he thought "woto" was a single word and that he did not clearly hear the verb involved. Conversely, a by-product of ITA has been an obvious improvement in the teachers' own pronunciation, since the children can write down anything they hear.

So much for the latest techniques. How does one make children *want* to learn to read in the first place, especially those from homes that place no value on books?

One answer to this can be found in the works of Sylvia Ashton-Warner, passionate books around which a cult has grown since their publication in the early 1960's. "I see the mind of a five-year-old as a volcano with two vents: destructiveness and creativeness," the author tells us in *Teacher*. "And I see that to the extent that we widen the creative channel, we atrophy the destructive one." To harness the creative vent, she recommended reaching into the mind of the child for the words that really mean something to him—words from his inner vision. These words, his private "key vocabulary," could then serve as a bridge to the writing of others.

"No time is too long spent talking to a child to find out his key words, the key that unlocks himself, for in them is the secret of reading," she declared. In a provincial New Zealand school, of which her husband was headmaster, Sylvia Ashton-Warner for twenty-four years successfully taught five-year-old Maori and white children to read and write by this "organic" method. She was an exceptionally gifted and intuitive teacher—this may have been a large factor in her success. Since she refuses to answer letters, many aspects of her work must remain unexplained. Americans who have tried to copy parts of her method report mixed results.

The two most powerful words in her classroom under any circumstances, she said, were "ghost" and "kiss"—any child, brown or white, always remembered these words from one look at them on the first day. A boy who had spent four months trying to learn such bloodless words as "come, look, and" from a standard Janet-and-John book took only *four minutes* to learn his own key vocabulary: "police, butcher knife, kill, gaol (jail), hand, fire-engine." Their "own" words reflected the drama, tears, love, and violence of life in the Maori village.

The vocabulary used in printed books for small children is necessarily a dead vocabulary, said Ashton-Warner, for although life is change, these vocabularies never change. When she first realized how alien and remote the middle-class white Anglo-Saxon primers seemed to her Maori pupils, she tried making another set of books from the immediate material in her class. "But all I did was to compose another dead vocabulary," she wrote later. "At last I know: Primer children write their own books."

Coming into her room at 9 A.M., these primer children would run to a large mat and look for their own words on cards which

Ashton-Warner had carefully tipped out from the children's individual cardboard folders, mixing them together before the pupils entered the room. The quarreling, concentration, and satisfaction involved in finding their own words was all to the good, she believed. When each child had collected all the words that belonged in his personal folder, he chose a partner and sat down to read him his words and to listen to his partner's. "And it is while they are teaching each other, far more effectively than I could teach them myself, that I call each one to me separately to get his new word for the day," she explained.

She would begin by having the child read her his old words. Any word he did not remember, she would destroy, because the word had failed as a one-look word and cannot have been of true importance to him. Then she would ask, "What are you going to have?" and draw him out in conversation until he suggested a word that appeared to have intense meaning for him. This she would print clearly in thick black crayon on a card made from cheap drawing paper, about a foot long and five inches high. He would watch her and say the word as she printed it in lowercase letters. Then he would trace the characters with his fingers (shades of Montessori) and put the word away in his folder.

"I look forward to the game with myself of seeing how nearly I hit the mark" (of choosing the right word for each child), wrote Ashton-Warner. Unlike the young New Jersey teacher, she had no trouble getting fresh words out of her pupils. After recess she would call on them again to see which of the new words they remembered, letting them keep only those. She thus made sure that when the children wrote their new words on the blackboard shortly afterward, they would be writing only words that carried with them an inner picture.

Though it might seem from all this that Ashton-Warner depended entirely on her version of the look-say method, the idea never occurred to her. Every afternoon she taught the chil-

dren their letters, she mentions in *Teacher*. She has never explained just how she proceeded with this task, probably because
it seemed too trite to mention.

After a child had a key vocabulary of about forty words that
he could read and write, and especially after his rate of intake
increased, she would promote him to the next group—the writers'
group. He might begin with just a two-word sentence, but soon
he would write much more, always about his own life: "Mummie
got a hiding off Daddy. He was drunk. She was crying." or "I
went to the river and I kissed Lily, and I ran away. Then I kissed
Philliga. Then I ran away and went for a swim."

He would also learn, to some extent, a general vocabulary that
sprang from all the children's writing, with such words as "then,
and, put, went, the, told, Daddy, Mummy, because."

What they wrote in the morning served as a set of graded,
brand-new stories for the children to read the rest of the day.
They would start out by writing their new words on the blackboard and taking turns in spelling them. ("This is a thing that I
hand to them: hearing each other spell," wrote Ashton-Warner.)

A quarter of an hour for spelling, another quarter-hour for
reading stories, another one for discussion. During the last quarter-
hour of the morning, the children in this group read what she
called Maori Transitional Readers—books she herself had prepared, using the cadence and vocabulary of Maori children's
speech to bridge the gap between their world and that of the
standard readers: "We play, eh?" "Me and you, eh?" "You stay
by me, eh, Daddy?"

Hearing the children read these, she said, was "a sound for
sore ears. Where has droning got to?" To find out, just get them
to read "Let us play," "Mother is in the house," or the conversation of Quacky the Duck: "I do not like the pond. I do not
want to live here." "Who in heaven—or in hell, for that matter
—speaks like this?" she asked. "*Cadence!* Has no one heard of

the word? Does no one read poetry? Why must reading be made harder for fives by the outlawing of cadence? I do not know, I do not know, I do not, I do not."

A five-year-old who meets words for the first time and finds that they have intense meaning for him will at once love reading, she declared. After a year of organic work his creative pattern will have been set—and even the static vocabularies may then be used without misfortune. Unlike so many Maori children on whom alien patterns have been imposed too soon, he will not bear a deep and permanent grudge against European education, nor turn inevitably toward delinquency.

Ashton-Warner's organic approach may prove particularly useful in reaching the children from our own slums, or ghettos, as it reached the Maori children. Yet she sees it as the answer to a larger problem: that of individual development in a mass culture. "The noticeable thing in New Zealand society is the body of people with their inner resources atrophied," she wrote. "They can buy life itself from the film and radio—canned life. And even if they tried to reach inward for something that maybe they could not find manufactured, they would no longer find anything there. They have dried up." Why had this happened, when the intention of modern education was just the opposite—to let children grow up in their own personal way, into creative and interesting people? she wondered. Where did the fault lie? Was it in the standard textbooks, in the teachers, or in the low-grade reading materials that were used so early in the children's lives? She was not sure what produced this deadly sameness in 999 persons out of a thousand. But she did know that, "as a rule, a five-year-old child is not boring. In an infant room it is still possible to meet an interesting, unpatterned person. . . . Therefore, the intent of the infant room is the nurturing of the organic idea, the preservation of the inner resources, the exercise of the inner eye, and the protraction of the true personality."

It can be no coincidence that, despite their many differences, some of the most successful methods of teaching reading to children—Montessori's, Moore's, ITA's, Ashton-Warner's—have one thing in common: They all enlist the child's creativity by letting him write his own words and stories almost from the beginning. They harness his own drive, avoiding standard primers like the plague. They let him proceed at his own pace, and so far as possible in his own way. Furthermore, each of these methods has proved effective with children well before they enter first grade.

Chapter 12

RAISING THE NATION'S

INTELLIGENCE

IF WE put enough energy, manpower, imagination, and money into it—if we dare go ahead—we can probably make the next generation of human beings far more intelligent than any that came before it.

This is not as unrealistic as it sounds. Physically at least, Japanese children of this generation tower above their parents, thanks to a better diet during their earliest years. Future generations of Americans might well grow to be much cleverer than we are, by as much as 20 to 30 points of IQ. What we need is a better intellectual diet for each child. And this we can provide, even with the fairly meager and incomplete knowledge we have today.

We can hook babies on learning, developing a life-long need for it. We can feed the toddler's drive to explore, allowing a variety of talents and interests to flourish. Through different kinds of responsive environments, we can let each child take the initiative in interesting dialogues that will lead him forward along the road of his choice. In well-baby clinics and pediatricians' offices, we can provide regular check-ups on intellectual development for every young child. By means of Children's Houses on every block, where mothers can leave the young for half an hour or a full day, and a network of home tutors, we can prevent the intellectual crippling of millions of youngsters.

In embryonic form or in isolated experiments, much of this already exists. However, a total program to increase the intelligence, artistry, and achievement of all young children would require an extraordinary effort throughout the nation, sweeping enough to overcome the Establishment's inertia.

Perhaps the nation is really ready for such change. As J. McV. Hunt points out, when men's reputations were made in the Roman Forum, the schools aimed at producing orators. When salvation seemed to depend on direct access to the word of God, the schools taught reading. Today's computers have increased the demand for people who can solve problems and use our symbol system; therefore the schools will have to produce such people. For this reason, he believes, the cognitive psychologists suddenly have a chance to make their voices heard over those of the Establishment.

Perhaps—but it won't be easy. At least three-quarters of a million persons must be found, and trained, if we want to provide enough teachers and teachers' assistants for the nation's three-to-six-year-olds (on double sessions.) This is more than six times the number of preschool teachers available today. Hundreds of thousands more teachers and aides must be found to launch any attempt to teach infants and toddlers at home, or in neighborhood Children's Houses. In addition, many of the 120,000 teachers and assistants who work with preschool children today may need retraining, to make them more cognitively oriented. Yet the very institutions that normally train such teachers are those most opposed to the new methods. Who, then, will turn the tide? It seems clear that Head Start's leaders will not take a stand on the matter. Nor can the U.S. Office of Education, despite the millions of dollars that flow through it, wield much influence on how the money is spent. For real change to occur, parents, interested professionals, and the general public will have to apply strong pressure on state and city superintendents of schools.

Some of the impetus for change will come from experts in fields other than education and psychology—men such as Dr. Paul Rosenbloom, a research mathematician who says he has "gradually been working my way down from graduate school to kindergarten," and has now at last reached the nursery level. Back in 1952, Dr. Rosenbloom was a professor of mathematics at the University of Minnesota, when he came to feel that many of the problems facing his graduate students had established their roots very early in life. He then began working in high schools, but was still dissatisfied; he switched to the fifth grade within a few months, going on to first grade and kindergarten some years later. Meanwhile, he developed an integrated mathematics curriculum for kindergarten through ninth grade in the MINNEMAST (Minnesota School Mathematics and Science) program. Probing still further, he is currently preparing a math program for three- and four-year-olds, and is hoping to bring together experts in such fields as languages, science, arts and crafts, to do the same for their subjects. After that, he'll concentrate on parents, for whom he'd like to write an unconventional handbook.

Unlike Spock or Gesell, who tell parents that they may expect certain stages at certain ages, and simply describe normal development, Rosenbloom would give parents little experiments to do— experiments from which the baby could learn something, while the parents gain clues to the best match for him. Some of these experiments would be taken directly from Piaget. For example, Rosenbloom might suggest that the mother reverse the baby's bottle before giving it to him, and then watch whether the baby can turn it around by himself to get at the nipple. Parents would never be told that this is supposed to happen at any particular age, but rather that when it does happen, here is the next thing to do. Active experimentation of this sort would be a source of fun for both parent and child. It would also accelerate the baby's formation of concepts.

To reach the parents of poorer children early in the game, Rosenbloom suggests using existing obstetrical clinics that conduct classes for parents. Until now, these classes have taught only how to feed, diaper, and physically care for the baby, but he believes one could easily insert some instruction in babies' thinking processes. Since many of these clinics have some mechanism for parents to come back for regular checkups of their babies, one could keep track of them for several years.

Dr. Rosenbloom sees nothing incongruous about educators getting involved in obstetrical clinics. Though half the nation's five-year-olds don't yet have kindergartens to go to, he foresees that educators will soon have to make plans for the newborn baby, the creeper, and the toddler, as well as children of nursery and kindergarten age. They may find themselves running battalions of home tutors, for example—a new breed whose function in education would parallel that of visiting nurses in public health.

In Washington, D.C., this has already begun, at least on an experimental basis. At the age of fifteen months, thirty babies in a poor Negro neighborhood received their first visit from a special kind of tutor who played with them intensively and encouraged them to talk. Every weekday from then on, the tutor spent a full hour alone with each baby in his home. They played guessing games, sorting games, counting games; they looked at pictures, read stories, blew bubbles—and all the time the tutor kept up a conversation with the baby, explaining what they were doing, labeling everything around them. It's a program of intellectual stimulation with focus on verbal skills, explains Dr. Earl Schaefer, the National Institute of Mental Health psychologist who started this Infant Education Research Project in 1965. One of its initial goals was to hook young children on books—to make books and stories so enjoyable for them that they develop a need for such things. Those behind the project hope to convert the statement "I know what I like," into "I like what I know."

A few years earlier, Schaefer had made a survey of research on intellectual growth which showed that, in every social group, the children's average IQ was set well before they entered school —and perhaps as early as three years of age. The question which then began to nag him was, Are we going to do anything about this insight? His answer was to start the home-tutoring project in cooperation with the Catholic University of America. First he recruited nine young women—all college graduates —who wished to go into the worst slum in Washington to help babies learn. Going from door to door in their chosen neighborhood for about two months, these young women found out where there were fourteen-month-old babies, and persuaded the mothers to join the program. Two tutors then began to alternate daily visits, so as to prevent the kind of attachment that might put them in the role of mother substitutes. One year after the tutoring began, the babies in the program, now at the age of twenty-seven months, scored between 10 and 15 points higher on the Stanford-Binet than did carefully matched controls. They did particularly well on the verbal items. The tutoring will continue until each child turns three, at which point he will be retested and, Schaefer hopes, placed in a nursery school.

Unfortunately, this program is rather expensive. Each tutor can take only four babies a day, to allow time for traveling from one home to the next and for daily discussions about each child's progress with the project's educational supervisor. Exclusive of

research costs, says Schaefer, it could run about $2,000 a child a
year, on a year-round basis. He points out that in areas where
enough volunteers can be found, the program requires only a
paid supervisor. In Maryland, for example, a group of volunteers
has started tutoring one-year-old babies in one of the state's
pockets of rural poverty. Each volunteer—usually a mature woman
who has raised her own children and now has spare time—gives
two hours of tutoring a week. Since they too alternate from day
to day, each baby gets four hours of concentrated attention each
week. Only a dozen babies benefit from this program, however,
and Schaefer believes it would prove impractical in an inner-city
slum, where the babies who need help would so greatly out-
number the available volunteers.

"No single approach can solve this problem," he declares.
"What we need is a revolution in education, to focus on the
child between one and three. We must put our resources into
early verbal development. We must create a new image of
woman, so mothers don't say apologetically that they're 'just a
housewife,' but take pride in their jobs as educators. We must
train new subprofessionals. Perhaps high-school girls could be
taught to work with babies. Perhaps day-care centers should be
placed right in the schools, so girls can learn to educate babies
and at the same time help working mothers. Whatever we do,
we need a public-health approach, to *prevent* deprivation rather
than try to correct it later. We need all kinds of programs—we
must develop a crusade."

With similar fervor and open-mindedness, Nancy Rambusch,
who sparked the recent Montessori revival, has started a pioneering "nursery-mat" in Mount Vernon, New York, within the
local school system. A nursery-mat, she explains, is as informal
and easily accessible as a neighborhood laundromat. Its official
name is the Child Development Center. Mothers bring their
three-to-five-year-olds in shifts, for only one hour each. While

these children attend their daily classes, the mothers are welcome to stay in another room with their younger offspring, where they can have coffee, talk, or use the new sewing machine. There are three adults—one certified Montessori teacher, one Montessori trainee, and one assistant—for each group of twelve to fifteen children, a ratio of 1 to 4 or 1 to 5. Yet despite the seeming restriction of this ideal ratio, the program reaches large numbers of children. With new shifts every hour, morning and afternoon, six adults can handle 125 children a day.

"There is no evidence that a two-and-a-half or three-hour program has any more payoff," says Mrs. Rambusch. "When you subtract the time spent on juice and cookies, toileting, outdoor play, and so forth, you only have about an hour and a half left in the regular nursery-school program anyway. This way, you need no diversionary tactics to calm the children down. And the teachers don't have to get into making Christmas stockings or Easter eggs, the really time-consuming things that have been the prescribed style."

During their precious hour, the children receive totally individualized teaching, she emphasizes. There is no group instruction whatsoever, since she believes it does not fit the child's development at that age. In a neat and quiet classroom the boys and girls busy themselves with toys of their choosing—Montessori puzzles, Cuisenaire rods, books, crayons. Some practice writing initial consonants with programmed materials put out by Science Research Associates. In the style of Ashton-Warner, each child has an envelope containing his own words, to which he may add every day. Knowing that they have little time and many interesting things to do, the children seem engrossed in their tasks or in their conversations with the teachers. At the end of the hour, they leave reluctantly, to be replaced by the next group.

While most of these children would qualify as poor, such a nursery-mat would prove marvelously helpful to youngsters of all

income levels. Two kindergarten teachers from a prosperous
Westchester suburb who observed the classes at the same time
I did said they were very impressed with the children's attentive-
ness and by the amount of work done with symbols. In their
own kindergartens, with older, middle-class children, they added,
they had never attempted so much. A nursery-mat would also
be a boon for the harried mother, offering her at least a brief
respite from the day's chores, together with congenial adult
companionship.

If a new flexibility seems to be emerging from these plans
and programs, so much the better. Much of the disagreement
about preschool education springs from the mistaken notion that
cognitive learning is an all-or-nothing business, robbing young
children of their childhood by leaving them no time to play. In
fact, it need take only a few minutes or an hour of well-chosen
activity each day. Never again in the child's life will so small an
investment in time produce such far-reaching results.

Furthermore, preschool teachers are discovering that they need
not adopt every aspect of any particular technique, so long as
they understand its goals. The day of the eclectic is approaching.
Though Mrs. Rambusch's nursery-mat has taken much from
Montessori, it is basically eclectic. In this sense, the most
prophetic voice around may well be that of Dr. Glen Nimnicht,
a Greeley, Colorado, educator.

Dr. Nimnicht boasts that he is "a first-class parasite—I've taken
whatever ideas I could from wherever I could find them." Pulling
together techniques invented by Omar K. Moore, Maria Montessori, and Martin Deutsch's group, he has formed his own program for both middle-class children and extremely poor Spanish-
Americans, and has planned his whole school as a responsive
environment.

Any time he wishes, a three- or four-year-old in Nimnicht's New
Nursery School may go to the Listening Corner (an idea borrowed

from Deutsch's Institute for Developmental Studies) and turn on a jukebox. He has up to twenty records to choose from, all cut right at the school: songs that incorporate his own name and the names of his classmates; stories from books that he can look at while listening (the jukebox button is literally tied to the matching book by a string); or simple tunes with pauses in them, during which the child can try to match certain sounds on a set of bell chimes.

No one except the head teacher ever initiates a conversation with a child, though all teachers are instructed to respond to a child whenever he speaks to one of them. This ensures that the topic will be meaningful to the child, who generally opens conversations with something vital, like "I saw something on TV" or "My dad beat me last night."

Montessori-style toys are in constant and concentrated use. There is a Reading Corner, where teachers read stories aloud, but only when they are asked to; this may sometimes go on for an hour or more, for one child or for several. The children stay with their chosen activities an amazingly long time. One of the poorest Mexican-Americans in the program, a little boy of four, painted seventeen pictures in a row shortly after entering the school. Another child spent his entire three-hour session absorbed in a picture lotto game, taking time out only for milk.

Once a day, when the child is not too engrossed in something else, he is invited to take his turn at playing with the typewriter. Copying Moore's early, nonautomated version of the talking typewriter, Nimnicht has set up four responsive-environment booths, each equipped with an electric typewriter, an exhibitor, and a blackboard. A college student acts as booth assistant. The child may refuse to go, and once there he may leave at any time, but he cannot stay in the booth longer than twenty minutes. By the end of their first year, about one-fifth of the children were able to copy their own stories on the typewriter, after dictating them to the assistant.

Formerly principal of a junior high school in Wyoming, in a valley with many impoverished Spanish-Americans, Nimnicht spent a couple of years at the Ford Foundation's Educational Facilities Laboratory, after which he decided to tackle the toughest job of all: the training of teachers. He now combines his post as professor of education at Colorado State College and the running of two demonstration schools: The New Nursery School, which opened in 1964 with help from a private foundation, and a similar Responsive Environment Nursery School, begun a year later for middle-class children whose parents could pay tuition.

He hopes to develop there a system that could be applied all over the country. To this end, he has concentrated on producing specific teachers' guides. He has also prepared some new tests of young children's progress in categorization, language, and other skills. With an eye to school budgets, he has kept the cost of his schools down to $500 a year per child (exclusive of research expenses), despite all their special equipment. He did not stint on the number of adults available (one teacher and one assistant for every fifteen children, plus a booth assistant for each talking typewriter), but he did make the schools run on double sessions and employ students who work part time, receiving low salaries since they are being trained. He believes that even a capable high-school senior can serve as a teaching or booth assistant in his system. One full-time assistant, a bright Mexican-American girl, does very well, even though her own education stopped at seventh grade.

For similar reasons, Nimnicht has not attempted to get an E.R.E. machine: Its $35,000 cost, he feels, would discourage or prevent widespread adoption of his program. His booth assistants can do almost anything the computer would do, he claims, and his booths cost less than $1,000 each, with a tape recorder and a Bell & Howell Language Master (which records words and phrases on cards that the child can play back) thrown in. This makes the talking-typewriter program financially feasible. In addition, working as a booth assistant is an invaluable form of teacher training.

When the New Nursery School's own graduates went on to Greeley public kindergartens, their teachers reported that, unlike other poor Spanish-American children in the school, these were doing as well as, or better than, average in their mixed classes. Even if the teachers believed this because they knew which children had attended the nursery school and thus expected these to perform better—which Nimnicht doubts—at least it shows, he says happily, that he has reversed the self-fulfilling prophecy. He adds, however, that the true test will come in the upper grades of school.

Nimnicht's missionary spirit has moved the Sumter, South Carolina, school system to launch a very ambitious program: It plans to open thirty classes for 900 children between the ages of three and six, all modeled on the New Nursery School, in an area that never had even a public kindergarten. At least one of these classes will be integrated. Before the first class opened, two teachers from Sumter spent eight weeks at Nimnicht's school in Greeley, being trained in responsive environments, and members of Nimnicht's staff went to Sumter to help in the planning. Since then, the New Nursery School has been sending out weekly teachers' guides and getting back reports on Sumter's progress. One week after the talking-typewriter booths were installed, for example, two Negro youngsters had learned to locate all the letters on the keyboard.

For men and women of imagination and fire, such as Rosenbloom, Schaefer, Rambusch, and Nimnicht, the educational scene has never been more promising. Research on early learning is expanding so rapidly that one can barely keep up with it. Though it remains anchored in the ideas of Piaget, Vygotsky, and Montessori, it is providing new models of its own. Pragmatists who can apply these models to actual teaching are increasingly in demand.

The new techniques they are devising may revolutionize more than preschool education. They may compel all schools to adopt some form of individualized instruction. For, once freed to advance at their own pace and in their own way, the youngest children will move so rapidly in certain areas that parents and teachers will attempt to preserve these gains through ungraded classrooms. The graduates of the new nursery schools and kindergartens will then become a powerful force for change throughout the schools.

The pioneers of early learning want to give every child a chance to develop his capacities to the fullest. Their techniques will increase man's variety, not reduce it. If they succeed, middle-class children will no longer be held back to some comfortable average—and poor children will no longer be crushed before they can learn to learn. Both will be allowed to find their own intellectual identities. Both will come closer to reaching their potential. This should make each human life more interesting, more productive, and more rewarding.

FOR FURTHER READING

Happily, since this is a reporter's book and not a scholarly treatise, I needn't list all the books and articles that I have consulted or that have some relevance to early learning. I will limit myself to those I found most valuable.

The list thus varies in length from chapter to chapter. In connection with Head Start, for example, there is nothing I can recommend. In other cases there are more research reports than full-fledged books, and sometimes the reports exist only in mimeographed form. The whole field is growing so rapidly that these titles represent a mere beginning, but I hope at least they will whet the reader's appetite for more.

Preface

Kirk, Samuel A. *Early Education of the Mentally Retarded*, Urbana: University of Illinois Press, 1958.

Suzuki, Shinichi, et al. *The Suzuki Symposium on Early-Childhood Education*, mimeographed report of week-long symposium, being published by the Music School of the Henry Street Settlement, New York City, 1967.

Chapter 1: The Battleground

Fowler, William. "The Effect of Early Stimulation in the Emergence of Cognitive Processes," in *Early Education: Current Theory, Research and Practice*, ed. by Robert D. Hess and Roberta M. Bear, being published by Aldine Publishing Co., Chicago, 1967. Comprehensive survey of recent research on early learning.

Kessen, William, ed. *The Child*, New York: John Wiley & Sons, 1965. An anthology that gives some perspective on how ideas about children have changed over five centuries.

Mead, Margaret, and Martha Wolfenstein, eds. *Childhood in Contemporary Cultures*, Chicago: University of Chicago Press, 1955. Perspective on different styles of child rearing.

White, Robert W. "Motivation Reconsidered: The Concept of Competence," *Psychological Review*, 1959, vol. 66, pp 297–333. (Also available as a chapter in *Functions of Varied Experience*, ed. by Donald Fiske and Salvatore Maddi. Homewood, Illinois: The Dorsey Press, Inc., 1961.) Description of parallel trends in animal behavior, psychoanalytic ego psychology and general psychology which lead to the concept of competence.

Chapter 3: The New Mind-Builders

Almy, Millie. *Young Children's Thinking: Studies of Some Aspects of Piaget's Theory*, New York: Teachers College Press, 1966. Describes recent conservation experiments in the United States; with a Foreword by Piaget.

Bloom, Benjamin S. *Stability and Change in Human Characteristics*, New York: John Wiley & Sons, 1964. Analysis of 1,000 longitudinal studies of growth.

Bruner, Jerome S. *The Process of Education*, Cambridge, Mass.: Harvard University Press, 1960. One of the most optimistic and readable books on education.

Hunt, J. McV. *Intelligence and Experience*, New York: Ronald Press, 1961. The bible of the cognitive psychologists. An analysis and interpretation of all the research on intellectual development available to 1961.

Hunt, J. McV. "Toward a Theory of Guided Learning in Development," in *Giving Emphasis to Guided Learning,* ed. by R. H. Ojemann and K. Pritchett, Cleveland, Ohio: Educational Research Council, 1966. Probes further into the problems raised in *Intelligence and Experience.*

Piaget, Jean. *The Origins of Intelligence in Children* (1936). New York: International Universities Press, 1952. Description of Piaget's own children and how their intelligence grew.

Piaget, Jean. *The Psychology of Intelligence* (1947). Paterson, N.J.: Littlefield, Adams & Co., 1963. A more theoretical book. Piaget's tortuous prose makes all his books heavy-going, and some readers may prefer starting with J. McV. Hunt's thorough explanation of Piaget's ideas in *Intelligence and Experience.*

Chapter 4: The Pressure-Cooker Approach

Bereiter, Carl, and Siegfried Engelmann. *Teaching Disadvantaged Children in the Preschool,* Englewood Cliffs, N.J.: Prentice-Hall, 1966. A revolutionary curriculum for disadvantaged children.

"Language Programs for the Disadvantaged," report of the NCTE Task Force on Teaching English to the Disadvantaged, National Council of Teachers of English, 1965.

Chapter 5: The Talking Typewriter

Moore, Omar K., and Alan R. Anderson. "The Responsive Environments Project," in *Early Education: Current Theory, Research and Practice,* ed. by Robert D. Hess and Roberta M. Bear, being published by Aldine Publishing Co., Chicago, 1967. Moore's most informative and up-to-date summary of his own work.

Chapter 6: The Americanization of Montessori

Fisher, Dorothy Canfield. *Montessori for Parents* (1912). Cambridge, Mass: Robert Bentley, Inc., 1965. Eye-witness report on the first Case dei Bambini.

Montessori, Maria. *Dr. Montessori's Own Handbook* (1914). New York: Schocken Books, 1965, with an introduction by Nancy Rambusch. Description of Montessori materials and techniques.

Montessori, Maria. *The Montessori Method,* (1909), New York: Schocken Books, 1964. The basic text on the subject, with an introduction by J. McV. Hunt.

Montessori, Maria. *Spontaneous Activity in Education*, New York: Schocken Books, 1965, with an introduction by John J. McDermott. First volume of The Advanced Montessori Method, a continuation of the preceding book.

Rambusch, Nancy McCormick. *Learning How to Learn: An American Approach to Montessori*, Baltimore: Helicon Press, 1962. The book that started the revival.

Chapter 7: Other Attempts to Halt the Downward Spiral

Deutsch, Martin. "Facilitating Development in the Pre-School Child," in *Selected Papers from the Institute for Developmental Studies: Arden House Conference on Pre-School Enrichment of Socially Disadvantaged Children*, reprinted by the Merrill-Palmer Institute in Detroit, Mich., from the Merrill-Palmer Quarterly, July, 1964.

Goldstein, Leo S. "Evaluation of an Enrichment Program for Socially Disadvantaged Children," mimeographed report by Institute for Developmental Studies, New York, 1965.

Gray, Susan W., Rupert A. Klaus, James O. Miller, and Bettye J. Forrester. *Before First Grade: The Early Training Project for Disadvantaged Children*, New York: Teachers College Press, 1966.

Gray, Susan W., James O. Miller, and Richard Hinze. *Demonstration and Research Center for Early Education: An Overview*, mimeographed report published by George Peabody College for Teachers, Nashville, Tenn., 1966.

Smilansky, Moshe. "Evaluating Educational Achievements," in UNESCO Educational Studies and Documents No. 42, 1961.

Smilansky, Sarah. *Progress Report on a Program to Demonstrate Ways of Using a Year of Kindergarten to Promote Cognitive Abilities*, Jerusalem: Henrietta Szold Institute for Child and Youth Welfare, 1964.

Sonquist, Hanne D., and Constance K. Kamii. "An Application of Piaget's Theory to Teaching in a Preschool for Disadvantaged Children," mimeographed by Ypsilanti Public Schools, Ypsilanti, Mich., 1966.

Weikart, David P., Constance K. Kamii, and Norma Radin. "Perry Preschool Project Progress Report," mimeographed by Ypsilanti Public Schools, Ypsilanti, Mich., 1964.

Chapter 8: Day Care: The Problem Nobody Wants to Face

Caldwell, Bettye M. "What is the Optimal Learning Environment for the Young Child?" *American Journal of Orthopsychiatry,* January, 1967.

Caldwell, Bettye M., and Julius B. Richmond. *The Children's Center: A Microcosmic Health, Education and Welfare Unit,* mimeographed report published by Dept. of Pediatrics, Upstate Medical Center, State University of New York, Syracuse, 1967.

Chandler, Caroline, and Reginald S. Lourie, ed., *New Perspectives in Early Child Care,* being published by Atherton Press, New York.

Mayer, Anna B., and Alfred Kahn. *Day Care as a Social Instrument: A Policy Paper.* A comprehensive mimeographed report published by School of Social Work, Columbia University, 1965.

Willner, Milton. "Day Care: A Reassessment," *Child Welfare,* March, 1965.

Chapter 9: The Discovery of Infancy

Bauer, Raymond A. *Some Views on Soviet Psychology,* published by the American Psychological Association, 1962.

Dennis, Wayne. "Causes of Retardation Among Institutional Children: Iran," *Journal of Genetic Psychology,* vol. 96, 1960.

Kagan, Jerome, and Michael Lewis. "Studies of Attention in the Human Infant," in *Selected Papers on the Research and Teaching of Infant Development from the 1964 Merrill-Palmer Conference,* ed. by Irving E. Sigel, reprinted from the *Merrill-Palmer Quarterly,* April, 1965.

Skeels, H. M. "Adult Status of Children with Contrasting Early Life Experiences," *Monographs of the Society for Research in Child Development,* vol. 31, no. 3, Serial No. 105, 1966. Follow-up of a famous 1939 study, confirming the importance of early stimulation.

Spitz, René A. "Hospitalism: An Inquiry into the Genesis of Psychiatric Conditions in Early Childhood," *Psychoanalytic Study of the Child,* vol. 1, 1945.

White, Burton L., and Richard Held. "Plasticity of Sensorimotor Development in the Human Infant," in *The Causes of Be-*

havior: *Readings in Child Development and Educational Psychology*, ed. by Judy F. Rosenblith and Wesley Allinsmith, Boston: Allyn & Bacon, Inc., second edition, 1966.

Chapter 10: The Hidden Curriculum in Language

Bernstein, Basil. "Language and Social Class," *British Journal of Sociology*, vol. 11, 1960.

Bernstein, Basil. "Social Class and Linguistic Development: A Theory of Social Learning," in *Education, Economy and Society*, ed. by A. H. Halsey, Jean Floud, and C. A. Anderson, New York: The Free Press, 1961.

Brown, Roger, and Ursula Bellugi. "Three Processes in the Child's Acquisition of Syntax," *Harvard Educational Review*, vol. 34, no. 2, Spring, 1964.

Cazden, Courtney B. "Some Implications of Research on Language Development for Preschool Education," in *Early Education: Current Theory, Research and Practice*, ed. by Robert D. Hess and Roberta M. Bear, being published by Aldine Publishing Co., Chicago, 1967.

Hess, Robert D., Virginia Shipman, and David Jackson. "Early Experience and the Socialization of Cognitive Modes in Children," *Child Development*, December, 1965.

Vygotsky, Lev Semenovich. *Thought and Language* (1934). Cambridge, Mass.: the M.I.T. Press, 1962. Introduction by Jerome Bruner.

Chapter 11: Early Reading

Ashton-Warner, Sylvia, *Teacher*, New York: Simon & Schuster, 1963.

Barton, Allen H., and David E. Wilder. "Research and Practice in the Teaching of Reading: A Progress Report," Reprint No. 388 of Columbia University Bureau of Applied Social Research, 1964. A critique of reading research.

Durkin, Dolores. *Children Who Read Early*, New York: Teachers College Press, 1966.

Flesch, Rudolf. *Why Johnny Can't Read*, New York: Harper & Row, 1955.

INDEX